GROWING
RHODODENDRONS
AND
AZALEAS

Geoff Bryant

CASSELL

Cassell Publishers Limited
Wellington House, 125 Strand
London WC2R 0RB

First published in Great Britain 1995
in association with
David Bateman Limited
Tarndale Grove, Albany Business Park, Bush Road
Albany, North Shore City, Auckland, New Zealand

Distributed in the United States by Sterling Publishing Co. Inc,
387 Park Avenue South, New York, NY 10016, USA

British Library Cataloguing in Publication Data
A Catalogue record for this book is available from the British
Library

ISBN 0-304-34677-2

Printed in Hong Kong by Colorcraft Ltd

Contents

The winter foliage of Kurume azalea 'Hino Crimson'.

Previous page: *R.* 'Trude Webster'

INTRODUCTION

Indica azalea 'Comptesse de Kerchove'

WELCOME to the genus *Rhododendron*, of which azaleas form two of the eight *Rhododendron* subgenera. These beautiful shrubs are so well known and widely grown that you probably already have a fair idea of what rhododendrons are, and how and where they grow. If you have ever visited a specialist rhododendron nursery, you will also be aware of the vast range that is available. The object of this book is to give you the information you need to get the best out of your rhododendrons and to increase your understanding and appreciation of these most beautiful shrubs.

I spend my time working with all manner of plants, yet I am always drawn back to rhododendrons. Why? There are of course the obvious reasons: beautiful flowers, magnificent foliage and an ability to grow in a wide range of climates. But more important, the more I look at rhododendrons the more I find things that I could not have dreamed of or that are not what I expected. Delight, surprise and intrigue probably sum it up. Delight because, although rhododendrons all seem so similar, each spring they reveal their differences with their beautiful flowers. Surprise because there is always something new:

a new hybrid, a new species, or just some minute feature. Intrigue because I know there's always something more to find out. Rhododendrons have a colourful and interesting history, complex interspecific and environmental relationships and are superb subjects for breeding programmes. They can be frustrating and confusing but they are hardly ever dull.

It is not surprising that the variety 'King of Shrubs' should be a rhododendron hybrid. Of all the garden plants, few genera seriously rival the rhododendron for the pre-eminent position. Roses may have more charm and a subtler beauty and many are in bloom for longer, but they cannot match the foliage and form of the best rhododendrons. Camellias are more compact, evergreen and come in a range of foliage and flower types, colours and flowering seasons, but they lack variety in form and colour when compared to rhododendrons. The magnolias may be as spectacular but most are too large for modern gardens; and most of them are deciduous.

Rhododendrons have it all, but unless you understand the basics of their development, cultivation and care the chances are that you will never really be aware of all they have to offer.

Opposite: *R. 'Bibiani'*

Chapter 1

HISTORY

R. degronianum

General classification and naming

MUCH of this book is taken up with a broad outline of the genus and its history. This may seem excessive but I make no excuses, because to grow rhododendrons well you need an understanding of the plants and their background.

And to know rhododendrons you have to know rhododendron species, and there are about 1000. Although you certainly don't need to be able to identify each and every one of them, it is essential to be familiar with the most influential because they crop up again and again as you look through the parentage of the garden plants.

Most of the important species were introduced into European and American gardens during the period 1790–1935 and the vast majority of the current garden hybrids have

been developed since 1900. There are species and hybrids in all sizes, shapes and colours. Once you appreciate how they are grouped and named and have a feeling for their history, everything else falls into place. A well-stocked rhododendron nursery can be daunting, but if you understand the significance of phrases such as 'it's a yak hybrid', 'it's a vireya' or 'it's a Belgian indica', you can largely predict how a plant will look and behave.

Species names

Modern botanical and zoological classification is based on the Linnean system. This was developed by the Swedish naturalist Carl von Linné (1707–78), who is more commonly known by the Latinised form of his name: Carolus Linnaeus. He refined classification to the extent that any living thing could be identified by just two names, and his system, still in use today, is known as binomial (two names) nomenclature. Binomial names are

Opposite: *R. calendulaceum*, the flame azalea, is a deciduous native of the eastern United States.

also known as proper, scientific or Latin names. Latin (and to a lesser extent Greek) has always been the language of scholars and scientists and is very useful because it is an international language.

The genus, the first name, is a grouping of closely related plants that share certain characteristics. The species, the second name, is a single plant type within the genus. So there can be many rhododendrons but only one *Rhododendron yakushimanum*. To qualify as a species a plant must be genetically stable and capable of reproducing true to type from seed. Natural or artificial hybrids, mutants and selected forms are not regarded as new species because they cannot naturally replicate themselves. If they are capable of natural replication yet can still interbreed with the species they may be considered as subspecies: naturally occurring, self-perpetuating variations. Subspecies (the name is often abbreviated to ssp. or subsp.) are usually geographical variations that occur after a population has been isolated for long periods.

R. schlippenbachii demonstrates that flower and leaf size are not everything.

The genera and species are the last links in a long series of divisions and subdivisions. For our purposes it is seldom necessary to look back further than the immediate wider family, the Ericaceae or erica family, but, as an example, the lineage as it relates to one species, *Rhododendron forrestii*, is as follows.

Phylum:	Plant Kingdom
Division:	Magnoliophyta
Class:	Magnoliopsida
Subclass:	Dilleniidae
Order:	Ericales
Family:	Ericaceae
Genus:	*Rhododendron*
Species:	*forrestii*

For most purposes a simple identification by genus (*Rhododendron*) and species (*forrestii*) is adequate. When written, the whole botanical name should be italicised. The initial letter of the genus name should be capitalised whereas the initial letter of the species name should be lower case. After the genus referred to has been clearly identified the name is usually shortened to the initial letter. This book, for example, is about rhododendrons so instead of writing the word out it is often abbreviated to *R.*, as in *R. forrestii*.

This may seem confusing enough, but because *Rhododendron* is a large and complex genus spread over a wide area, some grouping of similar species within the genus is also allowed. Our example, *R. forrestii*, is a typical small alpine species from Tibet, southern China and Burma; it may be placed, with others of its type, in a group known as a subgenus, which may be divided into sections and subsections. The complete description would be something like this; *Rhododendron forrestii* (subgenus Hymenanthes, section hymenanthes, subsection Neriiflora). In addition, rhododendrons have been extensively reclassified and it is common practice to include the classification under the old system. In this case: Balfourian series Neriiflorum, subseries Forrestii.

Variety and cultivar names

Natural hybrids or unusual forms may occur, and once a plant enters cultivation it is almost certain to be hybridised or developed in some way. Hybrids and cultivated forms fail the first test of a species — they cannot reproduce true to type from seed — so they must be classified in some other way.

Three terms are commonly used to describe these plants: variety (correctly *varietas*), cultivar and clone.

All garden plants are commonly called varieties, but the botanical definition is more precise. A variety is a normally non-self-perpetuating naturally occurring variation of a species, and is expressed as the abbreviation var., as in *Rhododendron forrestii* var. *tumescens*. When cultivated it may also be known as a selected form.

R. 'Jingle Bells'

By following our cultivar example, 'Jingle Bells', back to its species parents we can learn much about its behaviour and characteristics. This can tell you a great deal about the plant and is especially important when hybridising because it provides valuable clues about the potential results of crosses.

'Jingle Bells'	'Fabia'	*R. dichroanthum* ssp. *dichroanthum*
		R. griersonianum
	'Ole Olson'	*R. campylocarpum* ssp. *campylocarpum*
		R. fortunei ssp. *discolor*

This parentage provides numerous hints about the nature of the plant. A 'Fabia' background suggests orange flowers (by way of *R. dichroanthum*) and narrow pointed leaves (from *R. griersonianum*). The other parent, 'Ole Olson', may provide a touch of yellow (from *R. campylocarpum*) and may lead to more rounded foliage (through *R. fortunei*). But Halfdan Lem, the hybridiser, also posed interesting questions with this parentage: how would the large round leaves of *R. fortunei* combine with the long narrow leaves of R. *griersonianum*; and how would the dominant apricot-orange colour of *R. dichroanthum* be affected by the pink *R. fortunei*?

The end result is a plant that shows little *R. fortunei* influence, but which clearly states its *R. griersonianum* background. 'Jingle Bells' is very much an improved 'Fabia', with brighter colours, bigger flower trusses and healthier foliage. So although the influence of the 'Ole Olsen' parentage is not immediately apparent, a look into the background of 'Jingle Bells' soon reveals where the improvements over 'Fabia' came from.

R. 'Fabia'

Commonly used suffixes, prefixes and descriptive names

Names ending in um and us, the masculine form, may also end in a, the feminine form. Although it was officially ruled in the early 1980s that masculine endings should not be used, they are still in common usage.

Name	Definition	Example and reason
alba, albi, albo	Usually a prefix: white.	*R. albiflorum:* white flowers
anthum	Suffix: refers to the anthers or more commonly the flower as a whole.	*R. dichroanthum:* bi-coloured flower
arbor	Prefix: tree-like.	*R. arboreum:* tree-sized species.
auri	Refers to ears and indicates lobed leaves, flowers or some other part.	*R. auriculatum:* lobed flowers
aureus	Golden.	*R. aureum:* covered in golden hairs.
barbatum	Bearded, as in a seed or flower.	*R. barbatum:* hairy seeds.
brachy, brevi	Prefix: short or abbreviated.	*R. brevistylum:* short styled
calo, calli	Prefix: beautiful.	*R. calophytum:* beautiful plant.
calyx	Suffix: refers to the calyx of the flower.	*R. ciliicalyx:* calyx fringed with hairs.
campa	Usually a prefix: bell shaped.	*R. campanulatum:* bell-shaped flowers.
campy, campylo	Prefix: bent.	*R. campylocarpum:* bent fruit.
capitatum	Head-like, usually a reference to the flowers.	*R. capitatum:* flowers in a head.
carpa, carpum	Suffix: refers to the fruit or seed pod.	*R. cyanocarpum:* blue seed pods.
cephalum	The head, usually a reference to flowers in clusters, or heads.	*R. cephalanthum:* flowers in heads
ceras, cerasti	Cherry-red.	*R. cerasinum:* cherry-red flowers.
chamae, pseudo	Prefix: false, usually a reference to a plant of similar appearance.	*R. chamaethomsonii:* like a small *R. thomsonii*
chion	Snowy colour or texture.	*R. chionanthum:* snow-coloured flowers.
chroma, chryso	Golden, or bright, yellow.	*R. chryseum:* golden-yellow flowers.
ciliatum, cilii	Fine hairs.	*R. ciliatum:* leaves fringed with hairs.
cladum	Suffix: refers to the twigs or branches.	*R. orthocladum:* straight branches.
cola, icola	Suffix: indicates the habitat.	*R. rupicola:* found among rocks.
compactum	Having a compact growth habit.	*R. compactum:* a small plant.
complexum	Interwoven: refers to a densely twiggy growth habit.	*R. complexum:* dense twiggy growth.
cuneata, cuneatum	Wedge-shaped.	*R. cuneatum:* wedge-shaped seeds.
cyano, glaucum, caerulea	Blue.	*R. cyanocarpum:* blue seed pods.
dendricola	Of the trees, usually a reference to an epiphytic growth habit.	*R. dendricola:* no apparent reason.
dichro	Prefix indicates two forms or colours.	*R. dichroanthum:* bi-coloured flower.
discolor	Composed of, or found in, several colours.	*R. discolor:* several flower colour forms.
fastigiatum	Upright growth habit.	*R. fastigiatum:* no apparent reason.
ferrugineum	Rust coloured.	*R. ferrugineum:* red leaf undersides.
fimbriatum	Edged with minute hairs.	*R. fimbriatum:* leaves edged with hairs.
florum	Suffix: flowers.	*R. albiflorum:* white flowered.
folium	Suffix: foliage.	*R. myrtifolium:* myrtle-like foliage.
formosum	Beautiful. Not to be confused with formosanum meaning coming from Formosa (Taiwan).	*R. formosum:* large, fragrant flowers.
fulgens	Shining.	*R. fulgens:* shiny leaves.
giganteum	Very large growing.	*R. giganteum:* tree-like growth.
globi, globu	Prefix: round or globe-like.	*R. globigerum:* rounded buds.
grande, grandi	Large, may refer to the flowers or growth form.	*R. grande:* tree-like growth and large leaves.

Name	Definition	Example and reason
hirsutum	Hairy.	*R. hirsutum*: leaves with fine hairs.
insulare	Coming from an island.	*R. yakuinsulare*: from Yakushima Island.
intricatum	Tangled or twiggy growth habit.	*R. intricatum*: a dense, twiggy bush.
irroratum	Minutely spotted, as with dew.	*R. irroratum*: spotted flowers.
lacteum	Milky.	*R. lacteum*: creamy-white flowers.
lan, lani	Prefix: woolly.	*R. lanatum*: heavily felted foliage.
laxi	Prefix: drooping.	*R. laxiflorum*: loose open flower clusters.
lepidi, lepido	Prefix: scaly.	*R. lepidostylum*: very scaly foliage.
leuca, leuco	Prefix: white.	*R. leucaspis*: white flower scales.
longi	Usually a prefix: unusually long.	*R. longistylum*: flowers with long styles.
luteum	Yellow-coloured.	*R. luteum*: yellow flowers.
macro, mega	Prefix: large.	*R. macrosepalum*: large sepals.
magnificum	Impressive.	*R. magnificum*: large flower trusses.
meli, melia	Prefix: honey-like, a reference to the sap, nectar or scent.	*R. melianthum*: nectar-bearing flowers.
micro, mucro	Prefix: small.	*R. microphyton*: a small plant.
nigra, nigro	Prefix: black.	*R. nigropunctatum*: black-spotted flowers.
oides	Suffix: like or resembling.	*R. proteoides*: protea-like foliage
olea, olei	Prefix: resembling the olive (Olea).	*R. oleifolium*: olive-like leaves.
orbic	Prefix: circular.	*R. orbiculare*: rounded leaves.
oreo	Prefix: mountains.	*R. oreotrephes*: found in the mountains.
ovatum	Egg-shaped.	*R. ovatum*: egg-shaped buds.
pachy	Prefix: thick growth.	*R. pachysanthum*: heavy petals.
parva, parvi	Prefix: small.	*R. parvifolium*: small leaves.
pendulum	Indicates a weeping growth habit.	*R. pendulum*: drooping branches.
penta, quinque	Five, a reference to foliage or flower form.	*R. pentaphyllum*: leaves in fives.
peplum	Suffix: a coating.	*R. tephropeplum*: with a grey coating.
phyllum	Suffix: leaves.	*R. macrophyllum*: large leaves.
phyton	Suffix: plant.	*R. microphyton*: a small plant.
pilosum	Suffix: hairy.	*R. rubropilosa*: covered in red hairs.
poli, poly	Prefix: many.	*R. polylepis*: very scaly leaves.
pubescens	Pubescent or covered in small hairs.	*R. pubescens*: covered in fine hairs.
pumilum	Small or with creeping growth habit.	*R. pumilum*: a very small plant.
punctatum	Spotted.	*R nigropunctatum*: black-spotted flowers.
radicans	Rooting, usually referring to plants that strike roots as they spread.	*R. radicans*: a low, spreading bush.
repens, prostrata	Ground covering or very compact growth habit.	*R. forrestii* var. *repens*: low spreading bush.
reticulatum	Netted, or veined.	*R. reticulatum*: finely veined foliage.
rhoda, rhodo	Rose coloured or rose-like.	*Rhododendron*: deep pink flowers.
rigidum	Stiff.	*R. rigidum*: very twiggy growth.
rubi, russa, rubra	Red-coloured.	*R. rubropilosum*: covered in red hairs.
sanctum	Holy.	*R. sanctum*: found in a shrine.
sangui	Blood, usually a reference to flower or sap colour.	*R. sanguineum*: red flowers.
schizo	Split or found in two or more forms.	*R. schizopeplum*: has a split indumentum.

R. arboreum

Name	Definition	Example and reason
sepalu	Suffix: refers to the sepals.	*R. macrosepalum*: large sepals.
sphaero	Prefix: spherical or rounded.	*R. sphaeroblastum*: rounded buds
spila, spilo, spilum	Spotted or stained.	*R. spilanthum*: spotted flowers.
spinuli	Prefix: spiny.	*R. spinuliferum*: bristly new growth.
sulfurea, sulphureum	Sulphur coloured (bright yellow).	*R. sulphureum*: yellow flowers.
supra	Prefix: above or superior to.	*R. supranumbium*: found above the clouds.
telopea, telopeum	Conspicuous.	*R. telopeum*: bright yellow flowers.
tricha, tricho	Prefix: hairy.	*R. trichocladum*: hairy twigs.
verruco, verrucu	Prefix: covered in small wart like growths.	*R. verruculosum*: scaly leaves and flowers.
vestita, vestitum	Clothed or covered.	*R. vestitum*: felted leaves.
violaceum	Violet or purple.	*R. violaceum*: violet flowers.
virid	Green.	*R. viridescens*: yellowish-green flowers.
viscida, viscid	Prefix: sticky or covered in a sticky coating.	*R. viscidifolium*: sticky leaves.

Cultivar (a contraction of cultivated variety) and clone (vegetative replicas of the original cultivar) are somewhat interchangeable terms that refer to garden hybrids and forms. A name such as *Rhododendron* 'Jingle Bells' refers to a cultivar: a plant produced by crossing two distinctly different parent plants and capable of being perpetuated only by vegetative reproduction. When written, cultivar names are contained within single quotes (") and are not italicised. Also, in order to avoid confusion with species, such names should not be in Latin. Until the naming rules were standardised in 1958 there were many cultivars with Latin names; these still stand but new cultivars must have modern language names.

The origin of names

Botanists tend to observe conventions in plant naming, so if you know the basics and understand a little botanical Latin you can usually work out the derivation of rhododendron names. The name most often describes some feature of the plant, commemorates a person significant in its history or describes where it was first discovered.

Rhododendron means rose-coloured tree and is Latin derived directly from Greek: *rhodon* (rose) and *dendron* (tree). Species names ending in i, ii, ae, usually refer to a person, often the discoverer of the species. Our example, *Rhododendron forrestii*, was named after George Forrest, a famous explorer and plant collector.

Names ending in ense, ensis, ica or icum, refer to a location, hence *R. yunnanense* (Yunnan, China) and *R. japonicum* (Japan). The suffix anum can refer to a place or a person, so we have *R. yakushimanum* (from Yakushima Island) and *R. griersonianum* (after R.C. Grierson, a friend of George Forrest).

Names ending in a, um or us, such as *ferrugineum* (rust-coloured) or *arboreum* (tree-like), generally describe a characteristic. The suffix ifera, or iferum, means of, resembling, used for or bearing, which gives rise to names such as *odoriferum* (bearing fragrance). Yet other names describe colours: *alba* (white), *rosea* (pink), *rubra* (red) and *purpureum* (purple) are common examples.

Don't be put off by the seeming impenetrability of plant names; many of them are frequently used prefixes, suffixes and descriptive parts. The previous table defines some of the more common parts of names and provides examples of rhododendrons that use them.

R. arboreum 'Alba'

Rhododendron classification

Rhododendrons belong to the Ericaceae or erica family. Other familiar members of this family are the heaths and heathers (*Erica* and *Calluna*), mountain laurel (*Kalmia*), lily-of-the-valley shrub (*Pieris*), cranberry (*Vaccinum*), *Leucothe* and *Andromeda*. Almost all of the ericaceous genera make good garden plants. Several other genera are often associated with rhododendrons but they do not belong in the same family: *Camellia* is in the Theaceae, *Daphne* in the Thymalaeaceae and *Magnolia* in the Magnoliaceae.

With so many species discovered over several centuries it is perhaps not surprising that the genus *Rhododendron* has been revised several times. Currently the genus is divided into eight subgenera:

Rhododendron	Azaleastrum
Hymenanthes	Candidastrum
Pentanthera	Mumeazalea
Tsutsutsi	Therorhodion

The first four of these subgenera contain all but five species. Of the last four Candidastrum, Mumeazalea and Therorhodion each include only one species (*R. albiflorum*, *R. semibarbatum* and *R. camtshaticum* respectively) while Azaleastrum includes two species (*R. ovatum* and *R. stamineum*).

Subgenera Rhododendron and Hymenanthes include the plants that gardeners recognise as the 'true' rhododendrons. Some of these have small scales on their leaves, are known as lepidote rhododendrons and make up the subgenus Rhododendron. Species without leaf scales, the elepidote rhododendrons, form the subgenus Hymenanthes.

Subgenus Pentanthera covers the deciduous azaleas, and Tsutsutsi the evergreen azaleas.

Some of the subgenera are divided into sections, which are further divided into sub-

Opposite: *R. ponticum*, from the Hymenanthes subgenus.

Above: *R. sinogrande* is regarded as having the largest leaves of any rhododendron and is well worth growing for its foliage alone.
Below: The common deciduous azaleas, typified by this colourful group, are all included in the *Rhododendron* subgenus Pentanthera, which is a reference to their five anthers.

R. rubignosum

The genus *Rhododendron*

Based on the revisions of Cullen, Chamberlain, Sleumer & Philipson.

Subgenus	Section	Subsection
		Afghanica
		Baileya
		Boothia
		Camelliiflora
		Campylogyna
		Caroliniana
		Cinnabarina
		Edgeworthia
		Fragariiflora
		Genestierana
		Glauca
		Heliolepida
		Lapponica
Rhododendron	rhododendron	Lepidota
		Maddenia
		Micrantha
		Monantha
		Moupinensia
		Rhododendron
		Rhodorastra
		Saluenensia
		Scabrifolia
		Tephropepla
		Trichoclada
		Triflora
		Uniflora
		Virgata
	pogonanthum	
	vireya	Albovireya
		Euvireya
		Malayovireya
		Phaevireya
		Siphonovireya
		Solenovireya

R. lochae x R. christianae

sections. There are also groupings known as alliances and aggregates composed of very closely related species.

For many years the genus was grouped according to the Balfourian classification, named after its originator Sir Isaac Bailey Balfour (1853–1922), a professor of botany at Edinburgh University and one of the foremost rhododendron authorities of his day. His classification, which is sometimes still used in conjunction with modern revisions, divided the genus into 43 series that were further divided into subseries. Most of these divisions still have some relevance, but it has become obvious that many of the species could be grouped together, hence the development of the eight subgenera.

All this doubtless seems more than a little confusing, but it is not necessary to fully understand the classification system before attempting to grow rhododendrons. Do try at least to grasp the basic ideas of genus, subgenus, section and species. It will make your understanding of the genus that much more complete and it is a great aid to identification. Indeed, understand these points and everything else seems elementary.

Subgenus	Section	Subsection
Hymenanthes	hymenanthes (ponticum)	Arborea
		Argyrophylla
		Auriculata
		Barbata
		Campylocarpa
		Falconera
		Fortunea
		Fulgensia
		Fulva
		Glischra
		Grandia
		Griersoniana
		Irrorata
		Lanata
		Maculifera
		Neriiflora
		Parishia
		Pontica
		Selensia
		Taliensia
		Thomsonia
		Venatora
		Williamsia
Pentanthera	pentanthera	
	rhodora	
	viscidula	
	sciadorhodion	
Tsutsutsi	brachycalyx	
	tsusiopsis	
	tsutsutsi	
	tashiroi	
Azaleastrum	azaleastrum	
	species *R. ovatum*	
	chioniastrum	
	species *R. stamineum*	
Candidastrum		
species *R. albiflorum*		
Mumeazalea		
species *R. semibarbatum*		
Therorhodion		
species *R. camtschaticum*		

Azalea 'Martha Hitchcock'

What is an azalea?

Strictly speaking there is no such thing as an azalea, they are all rhododendrons. Originally, before evergreen azaleas were widely cultivated, the azaleas were classified separately from the rhododendrons on the basis of their deciduous habit and slight variations in flower structure, but as more plants were discovered and classified it became clear that the division was artificial.

As outlined above, the azaleas form two of the eight rhododendron subgenera. The deciduous azaleas make up the subgenus Pentanthera and the evergreen azaleas are classified under Tsutsutsi.

The division between evergreen and deciduous azaleas is not entirely straightforward. Deciduous azaleas are obviously devoid of leaves in winter and the foliage drop occurs entirely in the autumn. Most evergreen azaleas tend to hold their foliage through autumn, but by the end of winter they can be almost bare of leaves, especially in cold climates. Because evergreen azaleas can shed much of their foliage, botanists prefer to use the term persistent-leaved to evergreen for these plants.

Azalea 'Pearl Bradford Sport'

Deciduous azalea 'Anthony Koster'

Evergreen azaleas have two distinct types of foliage; they are dimorphic. Look closely at the foliage of an evergreen azalea as it develops through the growing season and the two forms will be readily apparent. The new growth that develops in spring is light in texture and quite a bright green. These leaves last through summer but begin to fall in the autumn and will carry on dropping through winter. The second flush of new growth that develops in summer and early autumn is of a heavier texture, is darker green and tends to persist through winter.

A trick sometimes used by growers to make their azaleas more evergreen is to prune off the first flush of growth. This removes the bulk of the leaves that would have fallen in autumn and also creates a more compact plant.

Special terms

Before we go any further there are a couple of terms that need to be explained, as you will come across them quite regularly.

Indumentum

Indumentum, or tomentum, is the felt or hair-like growth often found on the under-side of rhododendron leaves. Some species, such as *R. yakushimanum*, also show pronounced indumentum on the upper surface of the leaf but this usually wears off as the foliage matures. Many species exhibit a much reduced indumentum in the form of a dusty coating on the new growth.

The exact function of indumentum is unclear: it may serve as insulation against wind or cold or, as it usually persists on the under-side of the leaves where the stomata are

Rhododendron leaves with indumentum. The large leaf on the left is *R. macabeanum*. Top are 'Winsome' and 'Titian Beauty' and, centre, 'Hansel', *R. yakushimanum* and 'Pink Delight'.

Opposite: *R. scopulorum*

18

located, it may reduce moisture loss through transpiration. Species with young growth covered with indumentum are often coastal, so it may protect the tender growth from salt spray. Its function is probably a combination of these things, but whatever its natural value it certainly adds to the interest and beauty of many rhododendrons.

Novice growers often worry that the indumentum is some sort of disease, and they sometimes even go to the extent of rubbing it off. There would be few growers who do not recall at least one customer who brought in a perfectly healthy indumentum-covered leaf to have its 'disease' diagnosed.

Grex

Sometimes, particularly among British hybrids, you may come across the term grex. The word, which is Latin and means a flock, herd or troop, was used by hybridisers to describe groups of sister seedlings. Among the most famous of these groupings are the

R. 'Loderi King George' is from the Loderi grex developed by Sir Edmund Loder in England around the 1900s.

Loderi, Fabia and Naomi grexes. The plants within the groups are identified by the grex name and their own hybrid name, hence we have 'Loderi King George', 'Loderi Sir Joseph Hooker' and 'Loderi Venus'; 'Fabia', 'Fabia Tangerine', 'Fabia Roman Pottery'; 'Naomi Nautilus', 'Naomi Pixie' and 'Naomi Stella Maris' to name a few. Grex is sometimes abbreviated to g., as in 'Naomi' g.

Although group naming in this way is now officially discouraged, the grex was a useful idea. It automatically indicated the relationship between similar plants, something that is not always immediately apparent when every hybrid has its own completely different name.

How rhododendrons arrived in our gardens

Most rhododendron species are native to an area bordered by Pakistan in the west, central China in the north, southern India, Vietnam and Burma in the south and Taiwan in the east. This includes the classic Himalayan rhododendron areas of northern India, Tibet, Nepal and south-west China. Large groups also exist in Japan, Korea, South-East Asia, on the east and west coasts of North America, the Caucasus, southern Europe and the tropical regions of Malaysia, Indonesia, New Guinea and northern Australia.

The type of countryside and general climatic conditions vary enormously throughout this vast range. Specimens can be found growing in all sorts of unlikely places as well as in the moist woodland conditions that we tend to regard as typical of rhododendron country. Altitude, rainfall, temperature and forest cover are all important influences. If you are growing species, it is a very good idea to thoroughly research the natural habitat of the plant. Such knowledge can provide vital clues that will help you provide the ideal growing environment.

Most rhododendron species have been identified within the last 200 years. At the

R. burmanicum is typical of the somewhat tender yellow-flowered Burmese rhododendrons that enjoyed some popularity with hybridists in the 1930s and '40s.

time of Linnaeus the genus was well known but the number of species in cultivation was insignificant compared to the number we now know to exist. Within those 200 years rhododendrons have become one of the dominant garden shrubs, with a popularity rivalled only by the rose.

But the history of rhododendron cultivation goes back much further than 200 years. Chinese gardens have featured potted specimens for at least 2000 years, although it is unlikely that the Chinese practised hybridisation to any great extent. The evergreen azaleas, in particular those from Japan, probably have the longest history of hybridisation. The first recorded mention of specially cultivated plants appears around AD 750. In his book *A Brocade Pillow (Kinshu Makura)*, written in 1692 (not long after rhododendron cultivation began in Europe), the Japanese grower

Ito Ihei mentions several cultivars that had been grown for many years, and a few of these we can still see today. He also describes hybridising, grafting and other propagation techniques that are remarkably similar to those in use today.

R. hirsutum was probably the first species widely cultivated by western European gardeners. It is a native of the European Alps and was introduced around the mid seventeenth century. It was followed by the large and shrubby *R. ponticum*, the deciduous azalea *R. luteum*, and the small *R. ferrugineum*, a close relative of *R. hirsutum*. That virtually exhausted the range of local species; for greater variety it was time to look at the plants arriving from further afield.

Although we now acknowledge the greater Asian region as the main home of the genus, the first major influx of new species to arrive

R. luteum hybrid

R. niveum is fairly rare in cultivation and is a genuine case of a plant that deserves to be better known and more widely grown.

in Europe came from North America. Many were deciduous azaleas, such as *R. flammeum* (1789), *R. viscosum* (c. 1734) and *R. calendulaceum* (1806), which when crossed with *R. luteum*, a native of eastern Europe, produced the first hybrid deciduous azaleas. These plants enjoyed some popularity and the range of hybrids increased steadily, but they were scarcely a great sensation.

There are not many true rhododendrons native to North America but those that are generally show extreme hardiness. Of these, *R. catawbiense* (1803) has been very important. Its great hardiness (-30°C) and large trusses of flowers have had a considerable influence on many of the best hardy garden hybrids. Other American species, such as *R. maximum*, *R. macrophyllum* and *R. minus* have also been used in hybridising.

The eastern European species *R. caucasicum* arrived in Britain in 1803 as a gift to Sir Joseph Banks from Count Pushkin, a Russian horticulturalist and the father of the writer Aleksandr Pushkin. It was quite widely used in early hybridising and its influence is still seen today. When crossed with *R. ponticum* it produced 'Cunningham's White',

which was a popular cultivar in its own right for many years and is still extensively used as a grafting stock.

The first recorded European rhododendron hybrid was an azaleodendron (a cross between a plant of the Pentanthera or Tsutsutsi subgenus and a rhododendron). *R. periclymenoides*, an American azalea, was accidentally crossed with *R. ponticum* to produce *R.* x *hybridum*. The exact date of the cross is not known, but as the plant was given to the Royal Botanic Garden in Edinburgh, Scotland, in 1814, a date of around 1810 seems most likely. The first deciduous azalea hybrids date from a little earlier, with confirmed Belgian crosses from 1804.

As the direction of exploration shifted from the Americas to Asia, particularly the area from northern India through southern China to Japan, the range of known rhododendron species increased dramatically. The first Western botanical explorers in the Himalayas found the area to be a vast storehouse of rhododendron species and without doubt the modern centre for the genus.

R. russatum pink form is an alpine species from China.

The first Himalayan species to arrive in Europe was probably *R. arboreum*. It was discovered in 1799 and arrived in England in 1811. *R. arboreum* was an influential plant for several reasons. First, the true species has bright red flowers and was the first large-growing species of this colour to be used in hybridising. It brought a new brightness to rhododendron flowers.

Second, although basically red, the species often produces specimens with flowers in various shades of pink or white. This introduced an element of chance or genetic instability that has led to some strikingly marked plants.

Third, despite only being hardy to about -12°C it tends not to transfer this tenderness to its progeny when crossed with hardier species, so it introduced the possibility of combining bright colours with hardiness.

The next significant introduction was *R. campanulatum* around 1825. Although not greatly used in hybridisation *R. campanulatum* appears (in conjunction with *R. ponticum*) to have had a considerable influence in the development of mauve and purple cultivars.

The introduction of *R. griffithianum* in 1849 by Sir Joseph Hooker and of *R. fortunei* in 1855 by Robert Fortune (during an expedition to find new varieties of tea plant), were among the most important of the mid nineteenth century. The large-growing, fragrant *R. griffithianum*, a native of Sikkim and Bhutan, provided a boldness of foliage and flower that was previously unknown, though it lacked extreme hardiness and was inclined to be an untidy grower. *R. fortunei* from eastern China is an extremely hardy, fragrant, neat-growing large bush or small tree with magnificent foliage. Had *R. fortunei* been discovered first it is likely that *R. griffithianum* would not have had the influence that it did. Luckily it wasn't, because if it had been discovered first it might never have been crossed with *R. griffithianum* and we might never have seen the 'Loderi' rhododendrons that resulted.

Around this time the first of the tropical vireya rhododendrons were arriving in Europe. These plants, also known as malesian or Malaysian rhododendrons, will not tolerate frost and have to be treated as greenhouse plants in most temperate gardens. Nevertheless at the time the first species

R. javanicum is one of the most popular of the vireya rhododendrons.

were introduced greenhouse gardening was all the rage and because vireyas have very strikingly shaped and coloured flowers they were an instant hit.

Like many of the fashionable greenhouse plants of the nineteenth century, their popularity waned as hybridisers concentrated on hardy plants for outdoor use and as influential garden authorities emphasised naturalness in gardens. World War One saw the demise of all but a few of the large European private greenhouse collections, but in recent years vireyas have made something of a comeback. Where they can be grown outdoors, they are spectacular garden plants.

While rhododendron and deciduous azalea growers were primarily concentrating on producing hardy garden hybrids, the direction of evergreen azalea breeding was towards producing plants for greenhouses and for forcing into flower. This development was initiated by the introduction of *R. simsii* from sub-tropical Asia in 1808. *R. simsii* is a frost-tender species but it tends to produce double flowers, hybridises freely and can easily be forced into early flowering by giving it greenhouse conditions.

Belgian flower growers were the chief producers of the early *R. simsii* hybrids. This led to the plants being known as Belgian indica azaleas — indica meaning from the Indies, not a reference to *R. indicum*, a point that has caused confusion ever since. The tenderness of the tender Belgian indica azaleas led to evergreen azaleas being largely ignored as garden plants in Europe. However, in 1838, when they arrived in the United States, growers found that they were hardy enough to be cultivated outdoors in many southern states and they immediately became very popular.

R. lindleyi

R. simsii

The hardy and near-evergreen azalea *R. kaempferi* had originally been introduced to Europe as early as 1692, but it was largely ignored. Other hardy species from Korea, Japan and Taiwan, such as *R. yedoense* var. *poukhanense*, *R. kiusianum* and *R. nakaharae*, were much later introductions. They did not arrive until the late nineteenth to mid twentieth century, by which time the centre of evergreen azalea breeding had shifted to the United States. This combination of factors, together with a general unsuitability for the less reliable British climate, has led to evergreen azaleas being somewhat undervalued as garden plants in Britain although they are very popular elsewhere.

The period from 1830 to 1860 saw several vitally important developments for gardeners and botany. The first was improved and faster ships; second, the penetration of mountainous Himalayan and southern Chinese regions; third, the development of the wardian case; and fourth, the opening up of trade with Japan.

Transporting their finds back to Europe was always a major problem for the early botanical explorers. Even with ever faster and more reliable ships, transporting live plants was a very risky proposition. Most died on the journey, either through extreme variations in the climate or because of poor husbandry on the part of the ships' crews, which was mainly due to the lack of fresh water. The only alternative was to send seed to be germinated and grown on at its destination, which added years to the time between collection and the first flowering in cultivation, and was also unsuitable for cultivated specimens that did not reproduce true to type from seed.

R. lochae, a native Australian, is a heavy flowering bush inclined towards rangy growth.

over 45 kg of seed, which, considering the small size of rhododendron seeds, is a huge quantity.

It would be difficult to overstate the problems faced by the early botanical collectors. Getting to their destination, collecting and getting back out were all fraught with difficulty and danger. And nineteenth-century collectors, whose journeys were usually financed by nurseries, horticultural societies or private benefactors, were expected to be in the field for several years at a stretch — their financiers demanded value for money.

Collecting in the rhododendron belt of the Himalayas in the nineteenth century meant risking a hazardous sea journey to get there: pirates, storms and malnutrition were common at sea. There was the arduous overland trek that could run to several thousand miles there and back, always with the possibility of bandits and disease along the way. There were difficulties with the terrain, weather, wildlife and native politics before even starting to collect any plants or considering how to get them out. Several collectors perished on the job and most suffered from injuries or disease.

Most modern gardeners have no idea of the hardships that were endured to obtain what we now regard as common plants. The cynical would say that it was all done for money, and no doubt a successful new introduction could be worth a large amount, but it does not take much research to realise that most of the collectors were genuine enthusiasts, not gold-diggers. Which was just as well because they saw very little of the profits made from their endeavours.

Collecting in Japan was always thwarted more by political problems than by any transportation or climatic difficulties. The rhododendrons of Japan were not as exciting or as extensive as those of the Himalayan region but their potential was probably far more obvious. The heavy-flowering evergreen azaleas and the Japanese species of the Pontica sub-

The answer to this problem was the wardian case, which was effectively a miniature greenhouse or, as we would probably refer to it today, a terrarium. The wardian case was invented by a British cleric, Nathaniel Ward, who noticed small fern sporelings thriving in a closed bottle while all around them the grimy environment of industrial age Britain had killed far tougher plants. This ability of plants to survive and even flourish by recirculating the moisture and gases within an enclosed container was quickly exploited and before long even large specimens were being transported around the world in specially constructed cases.

There remained the problem of getting the plants to the ships, and most collectors still relied on seed as their main source of new plants. Successful seed collection meant being in the right place at the right time and it took hard work to harvest and prepare the seed for shipping. In one of his letters to J.C. Williams, the financier of his 1912–15 expedition, George Forrest mentions processing

section were clearly always going to be excellent garden plants and most were readily available; it was just a matter of being allowed to look for them and to take them out.

These problems were resolved by the actions of Commodore Perry in 1853 and the overthrow of the last Shogun in 1868. Japan was then open to exploration and, along with everyone else, the botanists and collectors were allowed in, and out.

Introductions continued steadily throughout the rest of the nineteenth century and into the early twentieth century. By 1930 most of the influential species were in cultivation, if not yet greatly used as parents for hybridisation.

The most significant twentieth-century introductions include *R. griersonianum* from Yunnan, China in 1917 and *R. yakushimanum* from Japan in 1932. *R. griersonianum* is a somewhat leggy and tender species with loose trusses of bright orange-red flowers. It was extensively used in hybridising for many years because its offspring tended to be very heavy flowering; unfortunately they also tended to become untidy growers with easily damaged foliage. Nevertheless many fine hybrids, such as 'Winsome', 'Anna Rose Whitney' and the 'Fabia' grex have *R. griersonianum* in their background.

R. yakushimanum has a compact growth habit and heavy-flowering tendencies extremely well-suited to modern small gardens. It was discovered as recently as 1920 and caused a minor sensation when first publicly exhibited at the 1948 Chelsea Flower Show. It is an almost perfectly formed dome-shaped plant that absolutely smothers itself in flowers and also has very distinctive foliage. The young growth is covered all over with a soft beige indumentum (felt-like hairs) while the mature leaves are deep green above, slightly rolled at the edges with

R. 'Anna-Rose Whitney' is an impressively large, heavy-flowering plant and a very popular hybrid.

a thick felt-like white to warm brown indumentum on the undersides. The species is hardy to at least -20°C and will tolerate some exposure to coastal conditions.

In recent years *R. yakushimanum* has become the darling of species fanciers and hybridisers. Its influence can be seen in many of the new compact hybrids and shows no sign of waning, and because it is also popular with species growers many selected forms are now available.

R. pachysanthum is a relatively new introduction that shows great promise, but it is unlikely that we shall see the discovery of any revolutionary new species. Nevertheless it has been a colourful and intricately interwoven history that has brought us to our current state of rhododendron growing. With so many species and hybrids to choose from, hybridisers will have plenty to work with for many years to come.

Chapter 2

RHODODENDRONS IN THE GARDEN

R. 'Lem's Monarch'

FEW gardeners grow rhododendrons exclusively or have only rhododendrons in their rhododendron areas. Massed plantings can be very impressive but they demand plenty of space and can be somewhat overpowering in a city garden. Most gardeners choose to use their rhododendrons within a wider garden design and fortunately rhododendrons are compatible with a wide range of common garden plants. You can use them in woodland gardens or alpine gardens and rockeries or as part of a well-stocked border or shrubbery.

Woodland

Small to medium-sized (50 cm to 1.8 m) rhododendrons usually look their best in a woodland setting. There are very few woodland perennials that are not suitable for cultivating with rhododendrons, although it is usually best to avoid those with aggressive roots, such as *Acanthus mollis*, or those with rapid spreading growth, such as *Ajuga reptans*. Wood anemones, primroses, hostas, and astilbes are ideal.

Using rhododendrons in a lightly shaded woodland is largely a matter of considering the height and spread of the plants, their moisture and sun exposure requirements, and then planting accordingly. Spacing is important because the ground under a rhododendron is heavily shaded and little will grow there. If your rhododendrons are planted too closely it will be difficult to establish a good cover of perennials; if they are too widely spaced it may be difficult to establish any continuity in the planting.

If you intend to divide your perennials regularly don't plant them where such disturbance is likely to damage rhododendron roots. Be careful with woodland bulbs as they will suffer if they have to compete with dense mats of rhododendron roots.

Opposite: Deciduous azaleas are often sold as unnamed seedlings. Provided you see the plant in flower before buying, that need not be a disadvantage, as this vivid orange seedling, seen with a Japanese maple, shows.

Evergreen azaleas tend toward soft pastel colours and generally blend well when massed, but care should be taken to avoid colour clashes when using them with deciduous azaleas.

Shrubberies

Many shrubs are suitable companions. The obvious choices are the other members of the Ericaceae such as *Pieris, Kalmia, Enkianthus, Andromeda* and *Leucothe*, but most plants with a preference for acid soil are also compatible. Camellias, the larger daphnes and most viburnums do well and are interesting in their own right. Where it can be grown well, *Crinodendron hookerianum* looks marvellous with rhododendrons.

Shrubs with very bold foliage, such as *Fatsia japonica* and the strongly variegated forms of holly (*Ilex*) or *Aucuba japonica* may tend to draw attention away from the rhododendron foliage. This effect can hide poorly foliaged plants but those with better foliage are best left without such brash competitors.

Berrying shrubs often make good companions because they provide colour at a time when the rhododendrons are usually at their least interesting. Red- or yellow-berried hollies blend well, although they can become rather large and may swamp smaller plants. *Skimmia japonica*, the *Sarcococca* species, *Ruscus aculeatus, Stranvaesia davidii* and the smaller cotoneasters crop reliably and do not mind some shade.

Rockeries

Dwarf and ground cover rhododendrons are superb rockery plants. Many of them are natural alpines that are perfectly at home under rockery conditions.

If the rockery is partially shaded, so much the better. The true alpines generally prefer half a day's sun, whereas the larger-leaved

Rhododendrons 'Scarlet Wonder' and 'Yellow Petticoats' are both at home in a large rockery or woodland garden and combine to provide a dramatic colour contrast.

dwarf hybrids are better with a reasonably bright but mainly shaded location. By varying the plants to suit the light exposure, you can grow a range of species and cultivars.

Rockeries and alpine gardens tend to be well drained and may, on occasions, be too dry. Always remember to add plenty of compost when planting and if there is any possibility of rapid drying, a few of the water-holding crystals normally used for pot plants wouldn't go amiss.

Shade

Many rhododendrons can be grown in full sun provided the soil conditions are good and they are not exposed to hot dry winds. Nevertheless plants grown in light shade tend to have larger leaves with darker colour and their flowers last longer, and in areas with hot dry summers shade is essential. Small-leaved alpine rhododendrons and most azaleas need to see some sun to keep their growth compact, but you will still need to shade them from the hottest rays to prevent the flowers fading too quickly.

Deciduous trees, especially those with a relatively light foliage cover make the best shade trees.

Most conifers and broad-leafed evergreens cast dense shade that causes plants grown under them to become drawn and leggy, but well-established evergreens that have had their lower branches trimmed and remaining foliage thinned, or the lightly foliaged evergreens like the vanilla tree (*Azara microphylla*) are often suitable. Avoid trees with masses of densely packed surface roots, such as willows and most birches, as it may be

R. 'The Honourable Jean-Marie de Montague'

difficult to get the rhododendrons established against such vigorous competition.

Old, high-branched oaks and maples are the ideal shade trees, but they are normally too large for domestic gardens. Japanese maples, magnolias and dogwoods are more appropriate for suburban gardens. *Liquidambar*, rowan (*Sorbus* species), *Robinia*, *Gleditsia* and *Styrax* are also suitable. The flowering cherries, plums and almonds (*Prunus*) are also first-rate choices, but take care when choosing *Prunus* as some tend to have dense surface roots.

Ultimately your choice of shade trees is more important than your choice of rhododendrons. If the shade trees are too densely foliaged or their roots are too greedy the rhododendrons will suffer. If the trees prove to be totally unsuitable they may have to be severely trimmed or removed entirely, which

can cause difficulties too. The rhododendrons may be damaged by the equipment used to remove the trees and they will certainly have to tolerate a greater exposure to the sunlight.

Take your time and choose carefully. It is not just a matter of the trees being attractive, they must also be functional. At a pinch you can scrape by with almost anything provided you are prepared to put in the work. But if you don't have to, why settle for second best?

Unusual growth forms and training

Most rhododendrons and azaleas develop into dome-shaped shrubs or small trees and are left to grow naturally, but some, particularly the more lanky rhododendrons and the evergreen azaleas, are suitable for training into more strictly controlled growth forms.

Satsuki azalea 'Chinzan' is a low-growing evergreen ideal for a rockery.

Ground covers and cascades

Dwarf rhododendrons often make very good ground covers. Plants such as the bright red 'Scarlet Wonder' and 'Elisabeth Hobbie' are ideal for covering an area while still providing a bit of height, but for truly prostrate ground covers you need to look at evergreen azaleas.

Evergreen azaleas are generally thought of as small, spreading bushes and many of them can be used as ground covers in the same manner as the dwarf rhododendrons, with the added advantage that they will strike roots as they spread. However, since the introduction of *R. nakaharai* and the North Tisbury hybrids in the 1960s and '70s it has been possible to get very low-growing, wide-spreading plants that are quite unlike other azaleas.

The North Tisbury hybrids were the first prostrate azaleas; they grow to about 1.2 m wide and generally have small red or orange flowers. If planted at the top of a bank or in a large pot they will also cascade. Newer hybrids have added to the colour range but it is still rather limited.

Espaliers

Espaliering is a good way to use plants that have attractive flowers but a growth habit that makes them unsuitable for garden use.

Tall and spindly rhododendrons, such as 'Fragrantissimum', *R. auritum* and *R. maddenii*, and upright azaleas, such as 'Fielder's White' and 'Orchid Gem' are well suited to espaliering. They are pinned to a wall or fence as they grow, and with regular tying back and trimming to shape they will develop a better foliage coverage than they would have as free-standing shrubs.

Standards

Strongly upright evergreen azaleas make good standards. The quickest method of producing a standard is to select a very young plant of an upright variety and train it from scratch. Start with unbranched cuttings and remove the side shoots and the lower foliage. Stake the plant as it grows and bush it up by removing the tip when it has reached the desired height, which can be anywhere from 50 cm to 1.2 m.

As the varieties suitable for use as standards tend to be somewhat frost-tender, this process is usually only suitable for potted plants that can be moved under cover or for areas that are close to frost-free.

Hedges

Hedges of evergreen azaleas are very popular in Japan, as are tightly clipped azaleas shaped into boulder-like forms. Making an

Above: *R. ponticum*'s dense growth, toughness and ability to withstand regular trimming make it a very useful hedging plant.
Below: Satsuki azalea 'Gunrei' may be used for a low hedge or border or as a potted plant. It is also ideal for bonsai.

azalea hedge requires no more than selecting a variety of the appropriate size and planting accordingly.

If the maximum number of flowers is required, trim the hedge immediately after flowering and give a tidy up just after midsummer. If a tightly clipped hedge is the aim, trim immediately after flowering and again in early autumn. This will sacrifice some of the flowers but will result in a more evergreen appearance over winter.

Some densely foliaged rhododendrons, most notably *R. ponticum*, can be used for shelter hedges. They will not withstand very heavy trimming but with regular clipping they can be kept reasonably compact.

Container growing

Rhododendrons, and in particular evergreen azaleas, are ideally suited to container growing. World-wide, millions of potted forced-flowered azaleas are sold each year for use indoors. Because of the shock of forcing and transplanting, many do not survive very long, but with the right treatment rhododendrons and azaleas can spend their entire lives in containers.

Although all rhododendrons can be grown in containers, very large specimens are usually better planted in the garden, simply because their bulk means they have to be grown in large and unwieldy containers. Any rhododendrons reckoned to be under 2 m high after 10 years' growth will make good container plants.

Always use a good quality potting mix, not your garden soil. Garden centres often have special rhododendron potting mixes that are slightly more acidic than the standard mix. Regular applications of mild liquid fertilisers and slow-release fertiliser granules should enable the plant to stay in the container for up to two years before repotting becomes necessary.

When the time to repot does arrive you have a choice; you can either move the plant

R. laetum, a popular vireya rhododendron.

up to a larger container, or undertake some light root pruning and repot it in the same container.

Regular root pruning will enable large plants to be kept in their containers and regular feeding and trimming should ensure that the foliage retains its normal appearance, rather than becoming dwarfed, as it would in a bonsai plant given similar root pruning. (Plants treated this way often flower very heavily.) The only limitation is the size of plant that you can handle; removing a large rhododendron from its comparably large pot for its biennial root pruning can be hard work, especially if you have several plants.

Because they often need winter protection, vireya rhododendrons are usually grown in containers. Many vireyas are natural epiphytes that grow high up in the trees of tropical rainforests. Use a very coarse potting mix that simulates the perfect drainage they would experience in the wild. An orchid or cactus mix blended with a little peat for added moisture retention is ideal.

Chapter 3

SOIL CONDITIONS AND NUTRITION

R. impeditum 'Blue Steel'

ALL the plants of the Ericaceae share a common trait that determines the conditions they require in order to thrive. They all have very fine, hair-like roots that form into a densely packed rootball that is seldom more that 60 cm deep but which is at least as wide as the plant. Understanding the root structure of rhododendrons is the key to growing them well; look after the roots and the rest of the plant will largely look after itself.

Why do rhododendrons have this type of root structure? Many rhododendrons have adapted to growing under deciduous trees, where they receive an annual dressing of fallen leaves and where the soil, over time, becomes composed almost entirely of leaf mould. This type of soil may not be high in nutrients but it is extremely high in humus and is moisture retentive yet well drained. It is not a deep soil (even if it were, the tree roots would remove many of the nutrients from the lower levels), but it is open and easily penetrated by fine roots, water and air.

This sort of compost-based soil is usually acidic, which is why rhododendrons have a preference for acid soils, even quite highly acid soils.

Under these conditions, rhododendrons have developed highly specialised roots. Most

This evergreen azalea shows the typical rhododendron root structure: a dense ball of fine roots that spread at least as wide as the plant while remaining confined to the topsoil.

Open woodland conditions, here under deciduous Japanese maples, are ideal for deciduous azaleas and naturalised bluebells.

plants have roots with very fine hairs at their tips. These root hairs, which absorb the essential minerals and moisture from the soil, greatly expand the surface area of the root tip. Rhododendron roots do not have root hairs; instead the very fine roots perform the functions of root hairs so that the whole surface of the root ball is composed of feeding roots. This enables rhododendron roots to make the best use of the small volume of soil they occupy.

What are the disadvantages of fine roots? Delicate hair-like roots are the first to suffer in periods of drought or flood, so steady moisture and good drainage are essential. Fine roots suffocate in compacted soils, cannot penetrate heavy soils and cannot move obstacles, such as large stones, that may obstruct their progress, so a loose, well-aerated, easily penetrated soil is essential. These requirements may seem excessive but they all come down to one thing: humus. It is virtually impossible to work in too much compost or

other humus-containing material if you intend to grow rhododendrons.

Alpine rhododendrons are better adapted to growing in mineral-based soils than in humus-rich leaf mould. However, they tend to occur naturally only in areas with fairly high rainfall and so are only rarely moisture stressed. The fine roots are an advantage in this environment too, as they enable the plants to make the best use of soils that are frequently leached of nutrients by rain and melting snow.

As mentioned earlier, many vireyas are epiphytes, and they generally only grow in rainforests or in areas that are frequently enveloped in cloud. Nevertheless they are more subject to moisture stress than other rhododendrons and do tend to have somewhat heavier roots as a result. Likewise deciduous azaleas, which can be found growing in quite dry environments, often have a few woody roots.

Grown under good conditions, rhododen-

R. 'Rubicon' has intensely coloured flowers and lustrous foliage.

drons are remarkably trouble-free. Apart from direct damage from wind, insects or sunburn, nearly all rhododendron disorders can be traced back to problems with the roots and ultimately the soil. Most gardeners underestimate the moisture and humus requirements and overestimate the need for supplementary fertilisers. If the plant has adequate moisture and a loose soil in which its roots can spread easily then little additional feeding will be required.

Preparation

Nothing improves the soil more than natural compost. It is both a fertiliser and a soil conditioner and adds the all-important humus that opens up and aerates the soil while retaining moisture. Visit any natural or artificial woodland area and look at the marvellous loose black soil that forms where the fallen leaves are allowed to build up and

decay; that is what your rhododendron soil should look like.

You really cannot overdo the compost; add as much as you can and dig it in as deeply as you can. Leaf mould, rotted conifer needles, rotted straw and garden compost are the best materials because they are full of vegetable humus and also provide good levels of nutrients. Stable manure and other animal manures are also good but they should be mixed with straw and well rotted. Peat, bark chips and rotted sawdust are acceptable but they tend to break down quickly, have little humus and are low in nutrients. Avoid mushroom compost as it is usually quite alkaline, which makes it unsuitable for most ericaceous plants.

Making your own compost is the best, and ultimately the cheapest, way of building up your soil's humus content and thereby improving its nutrient levels, aeration, structure, moisture retention and drainage. No garden should be without a compost heap and no serious gardener should be without compost.

The importance of pH

Moisture is filtered through the soil and the presence of minerals and vegetable matter in the soil will cause variations in its acidity or alkalinity. The precise measurement of these variations is known as the pH (potential of Hydrogen).

pH is measured on a 14-point scale based on the neutral point of pH 7. As the pH becomes lower (7–0) so the acidity increases, as it becomes higher (7–14) so the alkalinity increases. It is important to realise that this is a logarithmic scale, i.e., 6 is ten times more acid than 7, 5 is ten times more acid than 6 and so on. A pH of 4 is therefore 100 times more acid than pH 6. The same applies on the alkaline side: a pH of 10 is 100 times more alkaline than pH 8.

Rhododendrons prefer an acid soil with a pH in the range of 4.5–5.5, but most will grow perfectly satisfactorily with a pH as high as 6.5. Nurseries often sell simple soil test kits that will give a reasonably accurate guide to your soil's pH or you can get a rough indication by using litmus paper. Take a sample of the soil and dissolve it in water, then dip the litmus paper in the liquid. Blue litmus indicates alkalinity and pink to red indicates acidity.

Rhododendrons in the wild can sometimes be found growing on limestone, which is usually alkaline. However, lime is very soluble and usually travels downward through the soil, so if a humus layer builds up on top of the stone it may not necessarily become alkaline.

If you live in an area with limey soils it is possible to imitate this type of growth habit by constructing raised beds for your plants. The lime is unlikely to migrate upwards into a raised bed, whereas if you were to try and incorporate large amounts of acid soil into the existing limestone soil the lime would eventually seep back.

Nutrients

All gardeners know that plants require regular supplies of nutrients, and rhododendrons are no exception. Establishing the proper nutrient balance not only ensures that your plants will grow well, it also helps to make

Good rhododendron conditions are also ideal for many other woodland plants. Here, deciduous azaleas and forget-me-nots grow happily together.

them more resistant to climatic extremes, pests and diseases. However, rhododendrons have very efficient root systems and good soil with plenty of compost, combined with regular surface mulching will usually keep the plants growing well. Regular applications of mild liquid fertiliser and slow-release fertiliser pellets mixed into the mulch will overcome any minor deficiencies.

Plant growth requires certain elements (nutrients) be present in the soil. The main, or macro, nutrients are nitrogen (N), phosphorus (P), potassium (K), sulphur (S), calcium (Ca) and magnesium (Mg). In addition there are other elements that are essential but only required in minute quantities. The most important of these trace elements, or micro-nutrients, are iron (Fe), boron (B), molybdenum (Mo), manganese (Mn), zinc (Zn), copper (Cu), chlorine (Cl) and iodine (I). All

Be careful with fertilisers; this plant shows clear signs of burning due to the use of strong chemical fertilisers.

R. ciliatum

these elements are distinct from the essential carbohydrates, hormones, proteins, etc., that plants manufacture themselves.

Nitrogen, phosphorus and potassium are regarded as the 'big three'. You may have seen the letters NPK on fertiliser packets; this is a reference to the percentage of these elements in the fertiliser blend. A fertiliser with an NPK of 20.10.15 has 20% nitrogen, 10% phosphorus and 15% potassium by volume. You will also find listed the types of compounds in which the nutrient is available, such as nitrate or nitric nitrogen; potassium in nitrate, phosphate or chloride forms. This information is important in determining how quickly and for how long the nutrients will be available.

pH is also important in determining how efficiently soil nutrients can be used. In general, trace element deficiencies will be more apparent on acid soils, but very few soils are so acid that the effect is greatly noticeable unless the soil is regularly cropped. On the other hand, plants will have difficulty taking up iron and magnesium if the soil becomes too alkaline. A higher pH causes these elements to form compounds that make them unavailable to the plants.

Sources of nutrients

There are two main groups of plant fertilisers; organic and chemical, or to put it another way, natural and artificial. Both forms are available in dry and liquid forms. Dry fertilisers are almost always worked into the soil or used as a soil dressing. Liquid fertilisers are often applied to the soil too, but many are intended to be applied to the foliage. These are known as foliar fertilisers or foliar feeds.

Naturally occurring organic fertilisers, such as animal manures, tend to be relatively mild unless very fresh or applied in large quantities. Many have the benefit of adding humus as well as nutrients but some offer only a limited range of nutrients and with repeated use deficiencies may occur. You may need to add chemical fertilisers to ensure a good supply of all nutrients.

Although organic products are better at adding humus, chemical fertilisers are more suited to providing a balanced supply of nutrients and for correcting specific deficiencies. Chemical fertilisers come as general blends that supply a balanced blend of nutrients or as nutrient-specific fertilisers that supply one element or a selected group of elements. General fertilisers are ideal as a dressing before planting and as a booster in general cultivation, while nutrient-specific fertilisers are primarily intended to correct deficiencies. An example would be the use of iron sulphate or iron chelates to correct iron chlorosis.

Nutrient deficiencies

The most common nutrient deficiencies that occur with rhododendrons are a lack of nitrogen, and chlorosis caused by iron or magnesium deficiencies. Lack of nitrogen leads to slow growth and an overall yellowing of the foliage that affects the old growth first. Nitrogen is most effectively added by using urea, but this is a very strong chemical; use it at no more than 25 grams per 5 litres or severe, sometimes fatal, burning may result.

This evergreen azalea is exhibiting a bad case of chlorosis, note the badly discoloured foliage.

This rhododendron not only exhibits some chlorosis, it also has had its new growth damaged by frost.

Milder sources of nitrogen include ammonium sulphate and ammonium nitrate. Make sure these fertilisers are thoroughly watered in.

Chlorosis usually appears as yellow leaves with distinctly green veins. It indicates a lack of iron and/or magnesium. This may be due to deficiencies in these elements (more likely in container-grown plants) or to excess alkalinity preventing the plant from making the best use of the available nutrients.

It is often difficult for gardeners to tell the cause of chlorosis so aim to cover all possible causes. Mix about 20 grams each of iron sulphate and magnesium sulphate (Epsom salts) in 5 litres of water. Thoroughly soak the soil around the plants with this mixture. This will correct any deficiencies and the sulphate base of these fertilisers will help to neutralise any excess alkalinity.

Chelated iron is a faster-acting source of iron but is expensive and requires more care in its application.

Chapter 4

ASSESSING YOUR CLIMATE

Frost-covered *R. kiusianum*

BEFORE you start to think about planting you need to have an idea of the types of rhododendrons that best suit your climate. Obtaining accurate climatic information may be difficult. The local meteorological office can provide accurate data, but often at a considerable price. Almanacs and year books are a good source of information, but they tend to be very generalised. My advice is first to try to find out the minimum and maximum temperatures recorded in your area, as well as the average number and severity of frosts and the annual and monthly rainfall figures. The weather information in the local newspaper is a good place to start, or you might like to set up your own weather-recording equipment.

Once you have the basic climatic information, studying a few books or plant catalogues will enable you to eliminate the totally unsuitable plants and to make up a list of possible choices, bearing in mind the other considerations such as ultimate size and flower colour. The next step is to visit the gardens and the nurseries to see the plants. It is a great advantage to see the plants in flower before making your final choice. Looking at the real thing, rather than a picture in a book, will give you a far better appreciation of the plant even if it is not in flower. If you find a plant that appeals, ask the sales staff how it performs.

All this may sound very complicated and time-consuming but it is really only applied common sense. The alternative is the 'try it and see' method: buy a few rhododendrons that would appear to be of borderline hardiness for your area and see if they grow. If they do, you could perhaps try something more tender, if they don't, you'll have a better idea of the limits. It might take more time to do the research but it is probably cheaper.

Rainfall and temperature
Rhododendrons need moisture, not only soil moisture but atmospheric moisture. Alpines

R. crassum

will tolerate periods of very low humidity but in the main rhododendrons prefer moderate to high humidity, with regular rain and even soil moisture.

Rainfall data for your area is obtainable from your local meteorological office, climate tables in year books, or the weather page of your newspaper, but such raw data does not always tell the whole story. Just as important as the amount of rain is the way it is distributed.

If we look at some of the best areas in the world for temperate climate rhododendrons we can see that despite somewhat different rainfall patterns, they produce similar results.

The Pacific Northwest of the United States has a moderate rainfall. Portland, Oregon averages around 950 mm and it is evenly spread throughout the year. The rhododendrons are seldom subjected to drought but they may suffer from poor drainage in wet seasons.

The Otago Peninsula on the south-east of New Zealand's South Island experiences a slightly lower rainfall. Dunedin averages around 750 mm, but the rain falls evenly throughout the year and droughts are rare. Ireland and coastal parts of western Scotland experience very similar conditions.

Southern England is regarded as an excellent area for rhododendrons. Many areas experience quite low rainfalls (600–700 mm is common), but the rain often comes as mist and drizzle, so although little actual precipitation is recorded, the air and soil remain moist and cool.

The mid-altitude Himalayan home of many rhododendrons includes some of the wettest places in the world and the rainfall is sometimes very seasonal. Rhododendrons evolved here, however, and can cope with the variations. Also, generally excellent drainage and sloping ground means that the plants are rarely waterlogged.

Other areas with higher rainfall, such as the southern United States and the west of both of the main islands of New Zealand, are also suitable for rhododendrons but good drainage becomes increasingly important as the rainfall level rises.

Parts of south-eastern Australia, particularly around Melbourne, the eastern mountain areas, and Tasmania also provide good rhododendron conditions, although occasional droughts are common.

Rainfall cannot be looked at in isolation, temperature must also be considered. The effect of less rain can be offset by a slightly lower temperature and areas with higher temperatures can cope with more rain. A rainfall of 750 mm with an average temperature of 11°C in Dunedin (Otago, New Zealand) has much the same result as 950 mm at 12°C in Portland (Oregon, USA), while 1200 mm at 17°C in Sydney (NSW, Australia) is actually considerably drier.

Many alpine and cool-temperate climate rhododendrons prefer conditions like those of Dunedin and Portland. As you move into wetter and warmer climates, where high humidity is combined with high temperatures,

Drooping foliage, as shown here, and purple leaf spots are common reactions to cold winters.

it becomes increasingly difficult to grow alpines, although vireyas and low-altitude Himalayan and Asian species thrive.

There are no hard and fast rules, but as a general guide, areas with an annual average temperature above 13°C are likely to be unsuitable for alpines, especially if there is very high humidity in summer. All rhododendrons will be difficult to grow where the annual rainfall is less than 500 mm unless the climate is cool and cloudy and the humidity is high. Gardeners in areas that regularly experience summer temperatures above 32°C will struggle to grow temperate climate rhododendrons and high altitude tropical species may also suffer unless the humidity is high.

Frost

Rhododendrons vary considerably in their degree of frost tolerance. Some are completely intolerant of frost while others can withstand -25°C or lower. Most of the common garden plants will tolerate -5°C with many capable of withstanding -15°C.

If your local nurseries and garden centres value your trade they will be honest with you about plant hardiness, and they are probably the best place to start when it comes to actually seeing the species and cultivars that are best suited to your area. Parks and botanic gardens are also useful. However, you may find that unless your local gardens regularly make new plantings or specialise in rhododendrons, their selection may bear little resemblance to that stocked by the nurseries, which are where you are most likely to obtain your first plants.

Unlike many plants, choosing hardy rhododendrons does not mean that you must forgo the fancy cultivars — some of the best are also the hardiest. The range is such that apart from the vireyas and some of the more tender fragrant species, such as *R. nuttallii*, gardeners in cold climates are not greatly disadvantaged. However, it is up to you to make sure that any plant you buy is capable of

Even though many rhododendrons are very hardy, late spring frosts may destroy the flowers, as with this evergreen azalea.

Many evergreen azaleas, especially Kurume and Kaempferi hybrids, develop brightly coloured winter foliage. 'Johanna', shown here, is one of the hardiest and most colourful.

surviving, don't rely on nurseries and garden centres always to sell hardy plants.

A plant's hardiness is not absolute; local conditions, season, nutrient levels and the natural variation between individual plants all influence the chances of survival. There is also considerable variation even within a species, so although hardiness ratings are useful in eliminating the totally unsuitable plants, they are only a guide and no substitute for experience.

Frost damage can result from extremely hard short-duration frosts or long-duration moderate frosts, repeated freezing and thawing, and late frosts that occur when the plant is coming into new spring growth. There is not much you can do to change the minimum temperature apart from providing additional shelter, and late spring frosts are unpredictable, but you can reduce the effects of repeated freezing.

Very hardy rhododendrons tend to have sap that resists freezing, but the liquids in the stems of the more tender plants may freeze if the temperature drops too low. If this happens repeatedly, the bark begins to peel and the stems may split open, much like bursting a sealed bottle by freezing the liquid it contains.

Paradoxically, planting in a site that remains cold and shaded in winter can actually reduce frost damage by lessening the number of times the plant goes through the freezing and thawing process and the rate at which it occurs. Despite the fact that there is no firm scientific evidence that the rate at which a plant thaws has any effect on the damage it sustains, most experienced gardeners will tell you that if a frozen plant is exposed to the morning sun and thawed quickly it will suffer far more damage than one that thaws slowly.

Late frosts are by far the most devastating. Not because they are necessarily more damaging to the plants but because they tend to destroy the flowers and the new foliage, which are the most tender parts of the plant. If you commonly experience frosts after the spring equinox, it is vital that you provide some shelter, otherwise it is almost inevitable that at the very least the flower display will suffer.

If only light frosts are expected, shelter from the early morning sun may be all that is required. Growing your rhododendrons in woodland conditions not only provides a natural setting, the foliage canopy, however light, also protects the plants from frost damage. Shading may cause fewer flower buds to be formed but it ensures that those that do survive will bloom.

Plants in sites protected by eaves or tree cover will be considerably less exposed to frost than those out in the open. Temporary shelters and shadehouses with roll-down plastic covers can provide protection to about -6°C, but below that you will need to consider treating your tender specimens as greenhouse plants. Freezing winds can severely desiccate foliage and in very cold areas it may be necessary to wrap plants with hessian (burlap) as a protection against dry freezing winds. Bear in mind too that plants grown in containers may freeze solid if left outside, so choose really tough varieties for your outdoor containers.

Wind

Wind can burn the flowers and may damage tender spring growth. Young plants should be sheltered from strong winds, particularly in areas that are prone to hot, dry (föhn) winds. Fences, hedges and temporary shelters will all help young plants to get established. Rhododendrons tend to become more wind-resistant as they mature, although the flowers will always be likely to be damaged if exposed for more than a few hours.

Rhododendrons are seldom thought of as coastal plants as they tend to have a low tolerance of salt breezes. However, some species, such as the sought-after *R. yakushimanum*,

R. yakushimanum

occur naturally in coastal regions and will tolerate occasional salt spray. These species tend to have heavy indumentum, particularly on their young growth. This may protect the leaves from the effects of salt spray, but it is still a good idea to wash any salt deposits off the foliage. Coastal rhododendrons usually need shade, as the combination of salt breezes and sun tends to result in bleached and stunted foliage.

Chapter 5

CHOOSING PLANTS

R. 'Yaku Prince'

UNLESS you intend to create a specialist collection, such as rhododendrons of one geographic area or the work of a particular hybridiser, your choice of plants is largely a matter of deciding on size, flower colour, foliage and flowering season, while always considering your growing conditions. Other aspects may also be important, for instance you may want fragrance or a special growth form, but in the main it is size, colour and foliage that affect your decision.

Plant size

As with hardiness, plant size is enormously variable. Rhododendrons range from tiny rockery specimens like *R. nakaharae*, which takes many years to reach 15 cm high x 40 cm wide, to the tree-like species, such as *R. falconeri*, which can grow to 15 m in the wild. Most of the garden hybrids are in the 50 cm–2.5 m range, but there are plants of all sizes.

Deciding on the size of plant is not just a matter of knowing the height it reaches; the spread and the general growth habit are equally important. Most rhododendrons under 2.5 m high are wider than they are high, often by a considerable margin, so make sure that you can cope with the width of the plant as well as its height.

Densely-foliaged plants often look better than open growers but the more open plants allow light to penetrate and enable you to plant woodland perennials and small shrubs near them. Consider the overall effect — height, width and foliage cover — when deciding if a plant is suitable.

Flowers
Flowering season

Apart from the vireyas, which appear to be rainfall and temperature dependent in their flowering time, most rhododendrons have a fairly set flowering season. The exact flowering time of a particular species or cultivar will vary with the latitude and from year to

R. campanulatum

year, but the progression from early to late flowering plants through the course of the season is much the same every year.

Some rhododendrons are sensitive to temperature, and will flower after a prolonged exposure to mild weather, while others are more dependent on the lengthening spring daylight hours to initiate flowering. This is most evident in the evergreen azaleas: the early flowering Belgian indica hybrids will flower as soon as their buds are mature and often show the odd bloom in the autumn, but the late-flowering satsuki azaleas seldom flower until about a month after the spring equinox regardless of the temperature.

If you live in a mild frost-free climate you may find that the early flowering azaleas and rhododendrons can be relied upon to add colour from mid winter. But most rhododendron growers experience frosts in winter, which tends to make the early blooming plants something of a waste of time and effort. Even the hardiest rhododendrons have frost-tender flowers, few will tolerate lower than -2°C, so unless you can provide shelter for the tender blooms it is best to avoid the very early flowers.

By far the bulk of rhododendron flowering occurs in the six weeks after the spring equinox. It may be a little later in places with very cold winters and late springs but even so, most of the flowering will have finished well before the summer solstice.

Late-flowering plants are likely to have their blooms damaged by the increasingly strong spring and early summer sun. Some shading, at least from the hot afternoon sun, is vital if the blooms are to last. Those that flower late also have to compete for attention with the roses and early-summer blooming perennials.

By carefully selecting your rhododendrons so that their flowering season corresponds with the amount of shelter you can provide from late frosts and early summer sun it is possible, even in reasonably cold areas, to have a four-month flowering period. In frost-free climates this can be extended to up to eight months as many of the indica azaleas

Deciduous azalea 'Pink Delight' is a reasonably large bush that is best suited to a background planting or being massed with shrubs of a similar type and size.

R. 'Black Sport', developed from a chance find.

will start flowering in autumn and continue on through winter provided they don't get frosted.

Colour

There are rhododendrons in almost every colour and colour combination; all that is lacking is a true blue. There are plenty of mauves and purples that masquerade as blues but no gentian-blue rhododendrons.

Certain colours and styles of marking tend to predominate in each of the main divisions. Red, white, mauve and soft yellow are the predominant colours of the true rhododendrons, deciduous azaleas tend towards yellow, orange-red and red, while white and deep pink to magenta purple are the most common colours among evergreen azaleas. There are no yellow evergreen azaleas nor are there any deep blackish-purple azaleas, evergreen or deciduous.

Rhododendrons are either single colours or flushed with a secondary colour, often having contrasting spots in the throat of the flower that seldom develops into a conspicuous flare. Occasionally the flowers are edged with another colour.

Deciduous azaleas are often multi-coloured and frequently have very brightly coloured throat flares. They tend towards flushes of

R. 'Mrs G.W. Leak'

secondary colours rather than distinctly two-toned flowers.

Evergreen azaleas are frequently single colours with no contrasting markings, but many are very distinctly two toned, with clearly defined borders or with irregular flecks and sectors. They rarely have boldly contrasting throat flares.

Hybridisers have not failed to notice these differences and over the years many attempts at crossing between the groups to extend the colour range have been made. While we now know that it is genetically impossible to produce a natural yellow evergreen azalea by hybridising with yellow deciduous azaleas, it may be possible, if a little distasteful, to produce a genetically manipulated yellow evergreen azalea or a true blue rhododendron.

Deciduous azaleas tend towards oranges and yellows while evergreens are more commonly pink to mauve. Blending the two can lead to clashes — the pink evergreen azalea in the foreground of this group may be better replaced with a pale to mid yellow deciduous cultivar.

Colour combinations

With such a wide range of colours to choose from there is a very real possibility of combining colours that clash badly. The worst combination is probably the bright orange deciduous azalea with the intensely cerise evergreen azalea.

Remember to consider the flowering season. By planting specimens with differing flowering seasons together it may be possible to combine plants that would clash if they flowered at the same time.

Fragrance

There are many rhododendrons that possess at least some fragrance, yet one, 'Fragrantissimum', is far more widely known to the gardening public than any other. Obviously the name and the age of the cultivar (it was raised before 1868) have a lot to do with it. Unfortunately 'Fragrantissimum' happens to be the fragrant rhododendron that probably least deserves widespread recognition. It is a straggly, untidy plant that is really only suitable to growing as an espalier unless severely trimmed each year, yet it does have a spicy scent that can be overpowering.

'Fragrantissimum' is one of a group of rhododendrons known as edgeworthii hybrids because of the presence of *R. edgeworthii* in their parentage. *R. edgeworthii* is a species that occurs in north-east Burma, south-east Tibet, northern India and southern China at around 2000–4000 m altitude. In appearance *R. edgeworthii* is similar to 'Fragrantissimum' except that it has a felty indumentum and a

50

R. lyi

slightly stockier growth habit. The flowers are white-flushed-pink, as are those of most of its offspring.

Most of the *R. edgeworthii* hybrids were raised in the period from 1860–1890 and they tend to be similar to one another. Among the most common are 'Princess Alice', 'Countess of Sefton' and 'Suave'.

There are many other fragrant rhododendrons, such as *R. johnstoneanum* (and its double form 'Double Diamond'), *R. maddenii* (and its pure white form 'Virginalis'), *R. nuttallii*, *R. lindleyii* and *R. dalhousiae*, which was a parent of the very popular hybrid 'Countess of Haddington'. Lesser known species for the collector or connoisseur include *R. carneum*, *R. coxianum*, *R. decorum*, *R. formosum* var. *inaequale* and *R. lyi*. Most of the scented species are grouped in the Maddenia subsection but *R. edgeworthii*

is in the Edgeworthia subsection.

The fragrant rhododendrons mentioned so far tend to be slightly frost tender and are often damaged at -8°C. Fortunately the royal family of fragrant rhododendrons, the Loderi hybrids, are considerably tougher. They are magnificent plants that will tolerate temperatures down to -20°C or so. They are large bushes or small trees that will grow to at least 2.5 m high, so allow plenty of room.

The original Loderis were the work of Sir Edmund Loder and were introduced about the turn of the century. The cross — *R. griffithianum* and *R. fortunei* — has been repeated several times since, most notably by Lionel de Rothschild of Exbury fame, in the 1930s.

If the fragrant rhododendrons have any major failing apart from frost tenderness it is their restricted colour range. Most of them

R. pachysanthum has some of the heaviest upper surface indumentum of any rhododendron.

R. williamsianum has unusual rounded leaves, a feature that can also be found in many of its hybrids.

are white to pale pink with the occasional deeper pink such as the Rothschild hybrid 'Sheffield Park'.

R. johnstoneanum and its cultivated forms extend the range into the pale yellows but it is generally true that the more intense the colour the less intense the fragrance. This possibly just reflects the fact that brightly coloured flowers have little need to use fragrance to attract pollinators and fragrant flowers do not need colour.

Many deciduous azaleas are fragrant. Those with *R. occidentale* parentage, such as 'Delicatissima' and 'Exquisita', usually have golden yellow throat flares and are available in red and yellow shades, but most fragrant deciduous azaleas have white, pale yellow or light pink flowers.

Few evergreen azaleas have any noticeable scent. Those with a 'Mucronatum' background, such as 'Alba Magnifica' and 'Fielder's White' are usually lightly scented and can be very effective when mass planted. The colours are usually white to mauve.

There are also several fragrant vireya hybrids, most of which have *R. jasminiflora* somewhere in their parentage. These usually have long, tubular, white to light pink flowers.

Buds

The flower buds are often a very attractive feature and as they are usually clearly visible right through winter they ought to be considered when choosing plants. The buds can be rounded, pointed, tall or squat; they can be smooth, dusty or covered with fine indumentum; and best of all, they carry the promise of spring flowers.

Foliage

Regardless of how spectacular a rhododendron's flowers may be they are only there for a relatively brief time. In terms of the year-round appearance, the foliage is far more important than the flowers. Rhododendron foliage is every bit as variable as the flowers and can be just as beautiful too, so take the time to consider this when choosing your plants. While it is hard to ignore the foliage unless you are buying a deciduous azalea out of leaf, it is surprising how many people are prepared to overlook poor foliage for the sake of a month of pretty flowers.

Indumentum

Some gardeners find indumentum unattractive, but most feel it adds to the character of

Rhododendron leaves — from the huge *R. macabeanum* (bottom left) to the tiny leaves of *R. russatum* and *R. spiciferum* (bottom right).

R. 'Hansel' has thick indumentum on the undersurfaces, but, unlike *R. pachysanthum*, it rapidly wears away from the upper surfaces.

a plant. Many rhododendrons have indumentum but it is often restricted to the underside of the leaf and is seldom seen. It tends to be a feature that is more prevalent in species than hybrids, although *R. yakushimanum* hybrids are often well covered. Species with indumentum that could be considered a feature include: *R. bureavii, R. degronianum, R. pachysanthum* and *R. yakushimanum*.

The undersurface indumentum is more conspicuous with plants that can be looked up at from below. The Grandia subsection species, such as *R. grande, R. macabeanum* and *R. sinogrande*, all have very large leaves with a conspicuous silvery indumentum.

Size

Most rhododendron leaves are roughly oval in shape with rounded or slightly pointed tips. Leaf size, however, varies enormously. The smallest leaves are those of the alpine species and some of the evergreen azaleas, while the largest belong to the Grandia subsection species, which are natives of the very high rainfall areas.

Leaf size is usually closely related to plant size, rainfall and temperature. Tiny alpine species, such as *R. intricatum*, have leaves

as small as 10 mm long, but that is not surprising as they are only very small plants and could not support large leaves. Also, large leaves wouldn't last long in the bitter cold and high winds of the alpine zone.

The largest leaves belong to *R. sinogrande*, which when mature has leaves up to 75 cm long. These leaves are a glossy deep green, very leathery and heavily veined. Its rounded yellow flower trusses are very attractive but they pale into insignificance beside the foliage. Several other members of the Grandia subsection — *R. grande, R. macabeanum, R. magnificum, R. praestans* and *R. protistum* — have very similar foliage, but it is seldom more that just over half the size of a mature *R. sinogrande* leaf.

Sun tolerance

You will often hear it said that you can tell the sun tolerance of a rhododendron by the size of its leaves. To a large extent that is true; small-leaved plants will withstand more sun and often need some exposure, but it does not mean that for sunny positions you have to restrict yourself to plants with small leaves.

Sunburn, which usually appears as a browning in the centre of the exposed leaves, is far more severe in a very sheltered site or if the soil or atmosphere is dry. A plant with dry roots will eventually wilt, especially when exposed to hot sun or a dry atmosphere. Keeping the root zone cool and moist is paramount if you want to grow large-leafed rhododendrons in sunny positions, and this will help to raise the atmospheric moisture too.

If you suffer from high summer temperatures combined with low humidity, large-leafed species should be grown in light shade.

A cool, but not overly frosty, moist climate is the best for growing the widest range of foliage in the widest range of sun exposure.

Deciduous azaleas often develop rich autumn foliage colours.

Colour

Rhododendron leaves come in a variety of colours: all shades of green, often with purple, red or bronze tones. Alpines tend to have glaucous (bluish) or purple-tinted leaves, while those from mild, wet climates usually have the deepest green foliage.

The best colours are often seen in the new growth, which may be very bright and quite different from the mature foliage. This colouring, especially the silver tones, is often caused by a fine indumentum that wears away as the leaf ages. The reddish-brown pigment seen in young leaves is thought to afford the tender foliage some protection from sunburn. *R. protistum* var. *giganteum* and *R. nuttallii* are striking examples of red new growth.

Autumn colour

Deciduous azaleas often display brilliant autumn foliage colour. This starts as a yellowing and progresses through orange to bright red and finally deep blood red. The intensity of the colours is largely dependent on the autumn climate; warm days and cold, but not freezing, nights promote the best colour.

The spring leaves of evergreen azaleas also

colour before they drop. Some fall at the yellow stage but others turn red before dropping. The foliage that remains over winter is often intensely coloured and can be quite a feature. Azaleas with *R. kaempferi* backgrounds, such as 'Johanna' and 'Girard's Border Gem' usually show the best winter colour.

Scent

Some species have aromatic foliage. This may not be noticeable unless the foliage is crushed, but on damp or warm days the scent, often cinnamon-like, can be quite strong. *R. campylogynum*, *R. cinnabarinum*, *R. glaucophyllum* and *R. hippophaeoides* have noticeably aromatic foliage, as does the hybrid 'P.J.M.' ('P.J. Mezitt').

Bark

A few rhododendrons have a very attractive reddish-brown, peeling bark. It is rarely a feature to rival the flowers or foliage but it can add to the appeal of plants that might otherwise look rather drab in winter. Few hybrids have worthwhile bark, but several species show good colour. Some of the best are *R. barbatum*, *R. cinnabarinum*, *R. hodgsonii* and *R. thomsonii*. *R. arboreum* has a

R. 'Virginia Richards'

distinctive gnarled bark that sometimes peels to reveal a reddish undersurface.

Species or hybrids

It is common for rhododendron growers to become more enthusiastic about growing the species as they become more experienced. Most novices are initially attracted by the colour and form of the hybrids but come to appreciate the subtler charms of the species as the novelty of the fancy hybrids wears off.

The species offer just as wide a range of flower colours and foliage forms as the hybrids but finding all the desirable features in one plant is more difficult. That is why we have hybrids and hybridisers: to combine the best characteristics of the species in an ever-increasing range of new plants.

Finding species plants is often the most difficult part of growing them. Garden centres mainly stock fancy hybrids, so if you want species it usually means a trip to a specialist rhododendron grower or writing a letter to a mail order supplier of plants or seed.

You know that you are really hooked on rhododendrons once you start raising species from seed and find yourself marvelling over what most gardeners would regard as just a straggly weed with a pretty flower. Watch out, once it starts there's no turning back.

At the nursery

Having decided on the features that you want in your rhododendrons you need to be able to select good specimens. This is not really all that difficult because healthy plants usually stand out clearly. They are the ones with the lush, unmarked foliage and the even, well-branched shape. Reject any plants that have discoloured, undersized or damaged foliage, are obviously diseased or have uneven growth.

Plants that have been in their containers too long become pot bound and can be difficult to establish in the garden because they don't have many vigorous young roots. Plants that have very small leaves, long spindly branches or roots growing out the drainage holes of the container are usually pot bound and should be rejected. However, you may occasionally locate that rare or unusual specimen you have been looking for only to find that it is pot bound. If you can loosen the roots and provide plenty of water and feeding, such plants will usually recover and should not be ignored, especially as they are often sold cheaply to save the nursery having to repot them.

As far as possible make sure that the plant matches the description on the label as it is not unknown for plants to be accidentally mislabelled. Labels with colour photographs fade; they can be used as a guide but do not rely on them to be absolutely accurate.

Chapter 6

THE PLANTS

R. 'Bumble Bee'

THE plants listed here are chosen primarily because they perform well under a wide range of conditions, are useful and attractive, and I like them. They are not all available everywhere and they will not grow well in all gardens, but they are all beautiful, distinctive and well worth growing if your climate allows. The range of available rhododendrons is so large and varies so much from place to place that a large part of any plant list is going to be irrelevant for any particular reader. Also, plant lists date very rapidly as new cultivars supersede the old. Use this list as a guide, but remember, looking at the plants in your local nurseries and assessing them on the basis of your selection criteria is the only practical way to choose.

Interpreting the descriptions

Flowering season
This is divided into five categories: 1, late winter; 2, early spring; 3, mid spring; 4, late spring; 5, early summer. This indicates the start of the flowering season; the length of the flowering season depends on many factors, such as late frosts, wind, heat and sun exposure.

Size
The stated sizes (height x width) are for 10-year-old plants under average growing conditions. Rhododendrons grow throughout their lives and most plants will exceed the stated size, but under normal garden conditions it will provide a good indication of the size a plant can be kept to with occasional light trimming.

Hardiness
This is also divided into five categories:
1 = above -5°C
2 = -5 to -10°C
3 = -11 to -15°C
4 = -16 to -20
5 = below -20°C
Unseasonable frosts will usually cause damage at significantly higher temperatures.

Flower types

There are other flower shapes, such as tubular, but the vast majority fall into one of the four broad categories shown below:

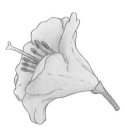

flat to saucer-shaped   funnel-shaped

campanulate   ventricose campanulate

Species

The true enthusiast would say that all rhododendron species are worth cultivating. However, many of the species are rather untidy, rangy growers that have little appeal for gardeners. The following are some of the more attractive, popular or influential species. Many more are available through specialist nurseries and rhododendron societies. The very rare species are often only available as seed.

R. arboreum (northern India to southern China)
Foliage: leathery, deep bronze-green, 175 mm long.
Flowers: deep red, white or pink, campanulate.
Flowers per head: 15-20.
Season: 1.   Size: 2.5 m x 1.8 m.   Hardiness: 3.

R. augustinii (southern China & Tibet)
Foliage: bronze-green, 100 mm long.
Flowers: bright lavender-blue, funnel-shaped.
Flowers per head: 2-6.
Season: 2.   Size: 2 m x 1.5 m.   Hardiness: 3, but very prone to damage from late frosts.

R. burmanicum (southern Burma)
Foliage: olive green, 75-100 mm long.
Flowers: bright chrome-yellow, ventricose campanulate.
Flowers per head: 4-6.
Season: 2.   Size: 1.2 m x 1.2 m.   Hardiness: 2.

R. calendulaceum — deciduous azalea (eastern North America)
Foliage: mid green, 100 mm long and conspicuously hairy.
Flowers: yellowish orange to flame red, funnel-shaped.
Flowers per head: 5-7.
Season: 4.   Size: 1.5 m x 1.8 m.   Hardiness: 5.

R. callimorphum (southern China to northern Burma)
Foliage: mid to dark green, glossy, 80 mm long.
Flowers: deep pink blotched red, campanulate.
Flowers per head: 5-8.
Season: 3.   Size: 1.2 m x 1.5 m.   Hardiness: 4.

R. campylogynum (southern China, Tibet & Burma)
Foliage: deep green, noticeably glaucous undersides, 25 mm long.
Flowers: variable, available in white, pink, red and purple forms, campanulate.
Flowers per head: 1-3.
Season: 2.   Size: 30 cm x 60 cm.   Hardiness: 5.

R. augustinii var. *chasmanthum*

R. catawbiense (eastern United States)
Foliage: dark green, shiny, 175-200 mm long.
Flowers: white, pink or mauve with greenish spotting, campanulate.
Flowers per head: 15-20.
Season: 4.   Size: 2 m x 1.8 m.   Hardiness: 5.

R. ciliatum (eastern Himalayan Region)
Foliage: deep bronze-green, glossy, fringed with hairs, 50-75 mm long.
Flowers: white flushed pink, campanulate.
Flowers per head: 2-4.
Season: 2.   Size: 1 m x 1.2 m.   Hardiness: 3.

R. cinnabarinum (eastern Himalayan region)
Foliage: bronze-green turning to glaucous greyish-green, glossy, aromatic, 60-80 mm long.
Flowers: brownish-red, waxy texture, ventricose campanulate.
Flowers per head: 3-5.
Season: 3-5.   Size: 1.8 m x 1.5 m.   Hardiness: 3.

R. dalhousiae (eastern Himalayan region)
Foliage: dark green, 175-200 mm long.
Flowers: greenish-cream to pale yellow flushed pink, fragrant, campanulate.
Flowers per head: 3-5.
Season: 4.   Size: 1.5 m x 1.5 m.   Hardiness: 3.

R. dauricum (south-east Siberia)
Foliage: deep bronze-green, 50-60 mm long.
Flowers: pinkish-purple, saucer- to funnel-shaped
Flowers per head: 1-2.
Season: 1.   Size: 1.2 m x 1.5 m.   Hardiness: 5.

R. edgeworthii (eastern Himalayas, southern China & Burma)
Foliage: dark green with a heavy buff indumentum, 75-100 mm long.
Flowers: white flushed pink, fragrant, saucer- to funnel-shaped.
Flowers per head: 2-3.
Season: 4.   Size: 1.2 m x 1.2 m.   Hardiness: 2.

R. elliotii (northern India)
Foliage: deep green, glossy, 175-200 mm long.
Flowers: deep red with darker spotting, campanulate.
Flowers per head: 9-11.
Season: 4.   Size: 1.8 m x 1.2 m.   Hardiness: 2.

R. fastigiatum (southern China)
Foliage: greyish green-glaucous, 20 mm long.
Flowers: bright lavender blue to purple, flat to saucer-shaped.
Flowers per head: 2-3.
Season: 2-3.   Size: 60 cm x 80 cm.   Hardiness: 5.

R. flammeum — deciduous azalea (eastern North America)
Foliage: mid green, hairy, 70 mm long.
Flowers: deep orange to bright red, funnel-shaped.
Flowers per head: 6-11.
Season: 4-5.   Size: 1 m x 1 m.   Hardiness: 5.

R. forrestii (Tibet, southern China & Burma)
Foliage: deep green, rounded, glossy, 40 mm long.
Flowers: bright red, ventricose campanulate.
Flowers per head: 1-2.
Season: 2-3.   Size: 30 cm x 75 cm.   Hardiness: 4.

R. fortunei (eastern China)
Foliage: mid green, 200 mm long.
Flowers: pale pink aging to white, fragrant, campanulate to funnel-shaped.
Flowers per head: 5-7.
Season: 3.   Size: 2.5 m x 2 m.   Hardiness: 5.

R. griersonianum (southern China & Burma)
Foliage: narrow, mid green with brown indumentum, 150-200 mm long.
Flowers: orange red, funnel-shaped.
Flowers per head: 5-12.
Season: 4.   Size: 1.2 m x 1.5 m.   Hardiness: 3.

R. griersonianum

R. haematodes (southern China)
Foliage: deep green with brown indumentum, 75 mm long.
Flowers: deep red, campanulate.
Flowers per head: 8-11.
Season: 2-3.   Size: 75 cm x 1 m.   Hardiness: 5.

R. impeditum (southern China)
Foliage: narrow, glaucous, 15 mm long.
Flowers: bright purple to bluish purple, flat.
Flowers per head: 1-2.
Season: 2-3.   Size: 30 cm x 50 cm.   Hardiness: 5.

R. indicum — evergreen azalea (southern Japan)
Foliage: narrow, mid green, hairy, 50 mm long.
Flowers: orange-red, funnel-shaped. 'Balsaminaeflora' is a double form.
Flowers per head: 1-2.
Season: 3-4.   Size: 1 m x 1.5 m.   Hardiness: 3.

R. irroratum (southern China)
Foliage: light green, 125 mm long.
Flowers: cream flushed and spotted pink, campanulate.
Flowers per head: 9-15.
Season: 2.   Size: 1.8 m x 1.5 m.   Hardiness: 4.

R. japonicum (syn. *molle*) — deciduous azalea (Japan)
Foliage: mid green, hairy, 75-100 mm long.
Flowers: yellow to orange-red, funnel-shaped.
Flowers per head: 7-12.
Season: 3-4.   Size: 1.8 m x 2 m.   Hardiness: 5.

R. johnstoneanum (northern India)
Foliage: bronze-green, slightly hairy,
Flowers: pale yellow, slightly fragrant, funnel-shaped. 'Double Diamond' is a double form.
Flowers per head: 3-5.
Season: 2-3.   Size: 1.2 m x 1.5 m.   Hardiness: 2.

R. kaempferi — evergreen azalea (Japan & Korea)
Foliage: deep green, slightly hairy, 75 mm long.
Flowers: pink to light red, funnel-shaped.
Flowers per head: 2-4.
Season: 3-4.   Size: 1.2 m x 1.5 m.   Hardiness: 5.

R. keiskei (Japan including Yakushima Island)
Foliage: bright green, pointed, 75 mm long.
Flowers: pale yellow, saucer- to funnel-shaped.
Flowers per head: 3-5.
Season: 2.   Size: 60 cm x 80 cm.   Hardiness: 4.

R. johnstoneanum

R. kiusianum — evergreen azalea (Japan)
Foliage: deep green, hairy, 10-20 mm long.
Flowers: purple, pink or white, flat to funnel-shaped.
Flowers per head: 2-5.
Season: 2-4.   Size: 50 cm x 1 m.   Hardiness: 5.

R. lapponicum (Scandinavia, Russia & Canada)
Foliage: deep green, 20-25 mm long.
Flowers: light purple, funnel-shaped.
Flowers per head: 3-6.
Season: 2.   Size: 40 cm x 60 cm.   Hardiness: 5.

R. leucapsis (Tibet)
Foliage: deep green, hairy, 50-60 mm long.
Flowers: white, flat.
Flowers per head: 3.
Season: 2.   Size: 50 cm x 80 cm.   Hardiness: 4.

R. luteum — deciduous azalea (Caucasus & eastern Europe)
Foliage: mid green, hairy, 100-125 mm long.
Flowers: bright yellow, funnel-shaped.
Flowers per head: 7-12.
Season: 4.   Size: 1.5 m x 1.5 m.   Hardiness: 5.

R. macabeanum (northern India)
Foliage: deep green, heavily veined with silver indumentum, up to 400 mm long.
Flowers: primrose yellow, ventricose campanulate.
Flowers per head: 15-20.
Season: 1-2.   Size: 3 m x 2 m.   Hardiness: 3.

R. nakaharai

R. maximum (eastern North America)
Foliage: deep green, glossy, 150-175 mm long.
Flowers: white to light pink with greenish spotting, campanulate to funnel-shaped.
Flowers per head: 15-20.
Season: 4-5.   Size: 2 m x 2 m.   Hardiness: 5.

R. nakaharai — evergreen azalea (Taiwan)
Foliage: deep bronze-green, hairy, 15-20 mm long.
Flowers: bright reddish orange, flat to funnel-shaped.
Flowers per head: 2-3.
Season: 5.   Size: 8-20 cm x 50 cm.   Hardiness: 4.

R. nuttallii (northern India, Tibet & northern Burma)
Foliage: deep green, slightly glossy, up to 300 mm long.
Flowers: creamy white, fragrant, very large, campanulate.
Flowers per head: 3-7.
Season: 2-3.   Size: 1.8 m x 1.8 m.   Hardiness: 2.

R. occidentale — deciduous azalea (western North America)
Foliage: mid green, slightly hairy, good autumn colour, 75-100 mm long.
Flowers: white to pale pink with a golden-yellow blotch, fragrant, funnel-shaped.
Flowers per head: 5-12.
Season: 3-4.   Size: 1.5 m x 1.5 m.   Hardiness: 4.

R. pemakoense (south-east Tibet)
Foliage: deep green, 20-30 mm long.
Flowers: pinkish-purple, saucer- to funnel-shaped.
Flowers per head: 1-2.
Season: 1-2.   Size: 25 cm x 45 cm.   Hardiness: 4.

R. ponticum (southern Europe to Iran)
Foliage: deep green, glossy, 150-200 mm long.
Flowers: light purple, funnel-shaped to campanulate.
Flowers per head: 7-15.
Season: 4-5.   Size: 1.5 m x 1.5 m.   Hardiness: 5.

R. russatum (southern China)
Foliage: deep green to bronze-green, 40-50 mm long.
Flowers: purple, pink or white, funnel-shaped.
Flowers per head: 4-10.
Season: 2-3.   Size: 1.2 m x 1.2 m.   Hardiness: 5.

R. sanguineum (southern China & Tibet)
Foliage: mid to deep green, silver-grey indumentum, 75-125 mm long.
Flowers: bright red, tubular to campanulate.
Flowers per head: 3-6.
Season: 3.   Size: 1 m x 1.2 m.   Hardiness: 4.

R. scabrum — evergreen azalea (Ryukyu Islands including Okinawa)
Foliage: bright green, 75-100 mm long.
Flowers: deep pink to red, saucer- to funnel-shaped.
Flowers per head: 2-6.
Season: 3.   Size: 1.2 m x 1.5 m.   Hardiness: 2.

R. schlippenbachii — deciduous azalea (Korea, eastern China & south-east Russia)
Foliage: mid green, 100-125 mm long.
Flowers: white to pale pink, funnel-shaped.
Flowers per head: 3-6.
Season: 2-3.   Size: 1.2 m x 1.5 m.   Hardiness: 5.

R. simsii — evergreen azalea (China, Taiwan, northern Burma & northern Thailand)
Foliage: bright green, hairy, pointed, 50-60 mm long.
Flowers: deep pink to red, funnel-shaped.
Flowers per head: 2-6.
Season: 2-3.   Size: 80 cm x 1 m.   Hardiness: 1.

R. sinogrande (southern China, northern Burma & Tibet)
Foliage: deep green, heavily veined with silver-grey indumentum, 400-800 mm long.
Flowers: cream to primrose-yellow, campanulate.
Flowers per head: 15-20.
Season: 2.   Size: 2.5 m x 1.8 m.   Hardiness: 3.

R. thomsonii (eastern Himalayan region)
Foliage: dark green, 80-100 mm long.
Flowers: deep red, campanulate.
Flowers per head: 9-12.
Season: 2-3.   Size: 1.8 m x 1.5 m.   Hardiness: 3.

R. viscosum — deciduous azalea (eastern North America)
Foliage: dark green, 50-60 mm long.
Flowers: creamy-white, fragrant, long-tubed funnel-shaped.
Flowers per head: 9-12.
Season: 5.   Size: 1.5 m x 1.8 m.   Hardiness: 5.

R. williamsianum (southern China)
Foliage: mid green, rounded, 40-50 mm long.
Flowers: light to deep pink, campanulate.
Flowers per head: 2-3.
Season: 2-3.   Size: 45 cm x 60 cm   Hardiness: 4.

R. yakushimanum (Yakushima Island off Southern Japan).
Foliage: deep green with a heavy white to buff indumentum, 50-100 mm long.
Flowers: white to pale pink, campanulate.
Flowers per head: 5-11.
Season: 3.   Size: 60 cm x 1 m.   Hardiness: 5.

R. yedoense var. *poukhanense* — evergreen azalea (Korea)
Foliage: mid green to bronze-green, slightly hairy, 80 mm long.
Flowers: pink to light purple, funnel-shaped.
Flowers per head: 2-4.
Season: 3-4.   Size: 1.2 m x 1.5 m.   Hardiness: 5.

R. zeylanicum (Sri Lanka)
Foliage: deep green, glossy, 100-125 mm log.
Flowers: bright red, campanulate.
Flowers per head: 15-20.
Season: 3.   Size: 2 m x 2 m.   Hardiness: 2.

Cultivars

Unlike the azaleas, rhododendron cultivars are not divided into recognised groups. They are most often simply referred to by their cultivar name. However, knowledgeable gardeners will often use the grex name or refer to a hybrid by its dominant parent. You may have heard such terms as *yakushimanum* or 'yak' hybrid, *williamsianum* hybrid or *griersonianum* hybrid. Hybrids of these and other species often closely resemble their parents in terms of foliage and general growth habit, although the flowers can vary markedly.

Dwarf bushes: less than 1 m high

These are very compact plants. Many of them only have small flowers but they are carried in great numbers. Very small rhododendrons often do better with half a day's sun. Grown in too much shade they tend to become drawn and their compact rounded shape is lost.

'Brickdust' (*R. williamsianum* x 'Dido' 1959)
Foliage: bright green, rounded, 40-50 mm long.
Flowers: pinkish-orange, campanulate.
Flowers per head: 2-5.
Season: 3.   Hardiness: 4.

R. 'Brickdust'

R. 'Curlew'

'Curlew' (*R. ludlowii* x *R. fletcheranum* 1969)
Foliage: bright green to bronze-green, 20-25 mm long.
Flowers: bright yellow, flat to funnel-shaped.
Flowers per head: 1-3.
Season: 2.   Hardiness: 4.

'Elisabeth Hobbie' ('Essex Scarlet' x *R. forrestii* var. *repens* 1945)
Foliage: deep green, bronze new growth, 40-50 mm long.
Flowers: deep red, campanulate.
Flowers per head: 4-7.
Season: 2-3.   Hardiness: 4.

'Ginny Gee' (*R. keiskei* 'Yaku Fairy' x *R. racemosum* 1979)
Foliage: deep green, 15-25 mm long.
Flowers: white edged and suffused mid pink, funnel-shaped.
Flowers per head: 4-9.
Season: 2-3.   Hardiness: 4.

'Patty Bee' (*R. keiskei* 'Yaku Fairy' x *R. fletcheranum* 1978)
Foliage: deep green, 15-25 mm long.
Flowers: soft yellow, funnel-shaped.
Flowers per head: 5-7.
Season: 2-3.   Hardiness: 5.

'Pematit Cambridge' (*R. pemakoense* x 'Blue Tit' before 1978)
Foliage: deep green 20-25 mm long.
Flowers: pale lavender, funnel-shaped.
Flowers per head: 2-5.
Season: 2.   Hardiness: 5.

'Scarlet Wonder' ('Essex Scarlet' x *R. forrestii* var. *repens* 1960)
Foliage: deep green, 40-50 mm long.
Flowers: deep red, campanulate.
Flowers per head: 4-7.
Season: 3.   Hardiness: 5.

'Shamrock' (*R. keiskei* x *R. hanceanum* 'Nanum' 1971)
Foliage: mid green, 20-25 mm long
Flowers: yellowish-green, funnel-shaped.
Flowers per head: 3-9.
Season: 2.   Hardiness: 4.

'Snow Lady' (*R. leucapsis* x *R. ciliatum* 1955)
Foliage: bronze-green, hairy, 30-40 mm long.
Flowers: white to cream, funnel-shaped.
Flowers per head: 3-5.
Season: 2.   Hardiness: 3.

'Sunup Sundown' ('Fabia' & 'Crest' background 1975)
Foliage: mid green, 40-60 mm long.
Flowers: red buds open pink and fade to pale pink, funnel-shaped.
Flowers per head: 3-5.
Season: 2-3.   Hardiness: 5.

R. 'Snow Lady'

Medium-sized bushes: 1 m to 1.8 m high

The cultivars in this size range are among the most popular. They are big enough to make an impact in a large garden but not so large as to take over a small garden.

'Blue Diamond' ('Intrifast' x *R. augustinii* 1935)
Foliage: bronze green, 20-30 mm long.
Flowers: lavender to mid blue, saucer- to funnel-shaped.
Flowers per head: 3-5.
Season: 2-3.   Hardiness: 4.

'Bumble Bee' (*R. ponticum* hybrid)
Foliage: deep green, pointed, 75-100 mm long.
Flowers: purple with very dark throat markings, funnel-shaped.
Flowers per head: 7-15.
Season: 3-4.   Hardiness: 5.

'Christmas Cheer' (*R. caucasicum* hybrid)
Foliage: mid green, 50-100 mm long.
Flowers: mid pink buds open pale pink and fade to white, funnel-shaped.
Flowers per head: 5-11.
Season: 1-2.   Hardiness: 5.

'Countess of Haddington' (*R. ciliatum* x *R. dalhousiae* 1862)
Foliage: bronze-green, glossy, 100 mm long.
Flowers: white flushed deep pink, fragrant, campanulate.
Flowers per head: 3-5.
Season: 2-3.   Hardiness: 2.

R. 'Blue Diamond'

R. 'Christmas Cheer'

'Dora Amateis' (*R. minus R. ciliatum* 1955)
Foliage: deep green, bronze new growth, aromatic, 40-60 mm long.
Flowers: white, funnel-shaped.
Flowers per head: 3-6.
Season: 2.   Hardiness: 5.

'Fabia' grex (*R. dichroanthum* x *R. griersonianum* 1934)
Foliage: mid green, pointed, 75-100 mm long.
Flowers: soft orange, campanulate. Several colour forms are available.
Flowers per head: 3-7.
Season: 3-4.   Hardiness: 4.

'Grace Seabrook' ('The Hon. Jean-Marie de Montague' x *R. strigillosum* 1965)
Foliage: deep green, pointed, 125-150 mm long.
Flowers: red fading at the edges, campanulate.
Flowers per head: 10-15.
Season: 3.   Hardiness: 5.

'Helene Schiffner' (*R. arboreum* hybrid 1893)
Foliage: deep green, 60-80 mm long.
Flowers: lavender buds open white, funnel-shaped.
Flowers per head: 3-7.
Season: 3.   Hardiness: 4.

'Hello Dolly' ('Fabia' x *R. smirnowii* 1974)
Foliage: mid green, buff indumentum, pointed, 60-80 mm long.
Flowers: reddish-orange buds open to yellow and light orange, funnel-shaped.
Flowers per head: 5-9.
Season: 3.   Hardiness: 5.

'Jingle Bells' ('Fabia' x 'Ole Olson' 1974)
Foliage: mid green, 60-80 mm long.
Flowers: deep orange buds open orange and fade to yellow, campanulate.
Flowers per head: 5-9.
Season: 3.   Hardiness: 4.

'Lem's Cameo' ('Dido' x 'Anna' 1962)
Foliage: deep green, glossy, bronze new growth, 80-120 mm long.
Flowers: apricot-pink and creamy yellow, funnel-shaped.
Flowers per head: 15-20.
Season: 3.   Hardiness: 4.

'May Day' (*R. haematodes* x *R. griersonianum* 1932)
Foliage: deep green with buff indumentum, pointed, 75-100 mm long.
Flowers: bright red, campanulate.
Flowers per head: 5-9.
Season: 3.   Hardiness: 3.

R. 'Helene Schiffner'

R. 'Hello Dolly'

'Nancy Evans' ('Hotei' x 'Lem's Cameo' 1983)
Foliage: deep bronze-green, reddish new growth, 60-100 mm long.
Flowers: orange buds open golden-yellow, campanulate.
Flowers per head: 15-20.
Season: 3.   Hardiness: 3.

'One Thousand Butterflies' ('Lem's Cameo' x 'Pink Petticoats' 1975)
Foliage: deep green, 100-125 mm long.
Flowers: deep pink with a pale pink centre and red spotting, funnel-shaped.
Flowers per head: 15-20.
Season: 3-4.   Hardiness: 4.

'Paprika Spiced' ('Hotei' x 'Tropicana')
Foliage: mid green, 75-100 mm long.
Flowers: cream with reddish-brown spotting and gold tones, funnel-shaped.
Flowers per head: 9-15.
Season: 3.   Hardiness: 4.

'Percy Wiseman' (*R. yakushimanum* x 'Fabia Tangerine' selfed 1971)
Foliage: deep green, 60-80 mm long.
Flowers: pale yellowish-pink flushed and edged pink, funnel-shaped.
Flowers per head: 13-15.
Season: 3.   Hardiness: 3.

R. 'Percy Wiseman'

'President Roosevelt' (unknown)
Foliage: deep green with a central yellow splash, 100-150 mm long.
Flowers: red with a white centre, funnel-shaped.
Flowers per head: 5-11.
Season: 2.   Hardiness: 4.

'Ring of Fire' ('Darigold' x 'Idealist' 1984)
Foliage: mid green, bronze new growth, 100 mm long.
Flowers: bright yellow flushed and edged orange, funnel-shaped.
Flowers per head: 5-11.
Season: 3-4.   Hardiness: 4.

'Rubicon' ('Noyo Chief' x 'Kilimanjaro' 1979)
Foliage: deep green, glossy, 75-100 mm long.
Flowers: deep red with darker spotting, campanulate.
Flowers per head: 9-17.
Season: 2-3.   Hardiness: 4.

'Sneezy' (R. yakushimanum x 'Doncaster' 1971)
Foliage: deep green with a slight silver-grey indumentum, 60-80 mm long.
Flowers: deep pink buds opening light pink with red spotting, campanulate.
Flowers per head: 7-11.
Season: 3.   Hardiness: 4.

'Suave' (R. edgeworthii x R. bullatum pre 1863)
Foliage: deep bronze-green, slightly hairy, pointed, 50-80 mm long.
Flowers: white flushed pink, fragrant, campanulate.
Flowers per head: 3-7.
Season: 3.   Hardiness: 2.

'Ted's Orchid Sunset' ('Purple Splendour' x 'Mrs Donald Graham')
Foliage: mid green, 100-150 mm long.
Flowers: deep lavender pink with orange-bronze throat markings, funnel-shaped.
Flowers per head: 7-11.
Season: 3.   Hardiness: 4.

'The Honourable Jean-Marie de Montague' (R. griffithianum hybrid before 1952)
Foliage: very dark green, narrow, 100-150 mm long.
Flowers: deep red, funnel-shaped.
Flowers per head: 10-14.
Season: 3.   Hardiness: 4.

'Titian Beauty' ([R. eriogynum x R. yakushimanum] x [R. yakushimanum x 'Fabia'] 1971)
Foliage: deep green with a slight silver-grey indumentum, 75-100 mm long.
Flowers: bright red, campanulate.
Flowers per head: 5-9.
Season: 4.   Hardiness: 4.

R. 'Titian Beauty'

'Unique' (*R. campylocarpum* hybrid 1934)
Foliage: deep green, 80-120 mm long.
Flowers: pink bud open pink and pale yellow
and fade to cream, funnel-shaped.
Flowers per head: 11-15.
Season: 2-3.   Hardiness: 4.

'Virginia Richards' ([*R. wardii* x 'F.C. Puddle'] x
'Mrs Betty Robertson' 1966)
Foliage: mid green, 75-125 mm long.
Flowers: orange buds open apricot orange with a
creamy orange centre, funnel-shaped.
Flowers per head: 9-13.
Season: 3.   Hardiness: 4.

'Winsome' ('Hummingbird' x *R. griersonianum*
1930)
Foliage: deep green, bronze new growth with
pale buff indumentum, 60-80 mm long.
Flowers: deep pink, campanulate.
Flowers per head: 5-9.
Season: 3.   Hardiness: 4.

'Yaku Prince' ('King Tut' x *R. yakushimanum*
'Koichiro Wada' 1977)
Foliage: deep green with a light tan indumentum,
80-120 mm long.
Flowers: light pink with red spotting, funnel-
shaped.
Flowers per head: 10-14.
Season: 3-4.   Hardiness: 5.

'Yellow Petticoats' ('Hotei' x ['Pink Petticoats' x *R.
wardii*] 1983)
Foliage: deep green, 75-100 mm long.
Flowers: bright yellow, funnel-shaped.
Flowers per head: 9-13.
Season: 3.   Hardiness: 4.

Large bushes: over 1.8 m high
Large rhododendrons can make a truly magnificent display but bear in mind that many
of the taller forms can develop into substantial trees.

'Anah Kruschke' (*R. ponticum* hybrid 1955)
Foliage: dark green, 100-125 mm long.
Flowers: reddish-purple, funnel-shaped.
Flowers per head: 7-12.
Season: 4.   Size: 2 m x 2 m.   Hardiness: 5.

Above: *R. 'Virginia Richards'*
Below: *R. 'Yellow Petticoats'*

Above: *R. 'Cornubia'*
Below: *R. 'Fastuosum Flore Pleno'*

'Anna' ('Norman Gill' x 'The Hon. Jean-Marie de Montague' 1952)
Foliage: deep green, narrow, 125-175 mm long.
Flowers: Red buds open to deep pink with red throat markings and fade to pale pink, funnel-shaped.
Flowers per head: 7-12.
Season: 3-4.   Size: 2 m x 2 m.   Hardiness: 4.

'Anna-Rose Whitney' (*R. griersonianum* x 'Countess of Derby' 1954)
Foliage: mid green, rounded, 150-200 mm long.
Flowers: deep pink, trumpet-shaped.
Flowers per head: 7-12.
Season: 4.   Size: 3 m x 3 m.   Hardiness: 4.

'Babylon' (*R. calophytum* x *R. praevernum* 1955)
Foliage: deep green, narrow, 100-150 mm long.
Flowers: white to pale pink with deep brown throat markings, funnel-shaped.
Flowers per head: 9-15.
Season: 2.   Size: 2.5 m x 2.5 m.   Hardiness: 5.

'Bibiani' ('Moser's Maroon' x *R. arboreum* 1934)
Foliage: dark green, glossy, 125-175 mm long.
Flowers: deep red, campanulate to funnel-shaped.
Flowers per head: 11-15.
Season: 2.   Size: 2.5 m x 2.5 m.   Hardiness: 3.

'Cornubia' (*R. arboreum* x 'Shilsonii' before 1912)
Foliage: mid green, 80-140 mm long.
Flowers: bright red, campanulate to funnel-shaped.
Flowers per head: 7-11.
Season: 1-2.   Size: 2.5 m x 2 m.   Hardiness: 2.

'Faggeter's Favourite' (*R. fortunei* hybrid 1933)
Foliage: mid green, 125-175 mm long.
Flowers: cream flushed light pink with darker markings, mildly fragrant, funnel-shaped.
Flowers per head: 7-11.
Season: 3.   Size: 2.5 m x 2.5 m.   Hardiness: 4.

'Fastuosum Flore Pleno' (*R. catawbiense* x *R. ponticum* before 1846)
Foliage: mid green, 100-150 mm long.
Flowers: deep lavender with greenish-yellow throat markings, semi-double.
Flowers per head: 7-15.
Season: 3-4.   Size: 2.5 m x 2.5 m.   Hardiness: 5.

'Fragrantissimum' (*R. edgeworthii* x *R. formosum* 1868)
Foliage: deep bronze green, pointed, 75-100 mm long.
Flowers: white flushed pink, highly fragrant, funnel-shaped.
Flowers per head: 3-7.
Season: 3.   Size: 2 m x 2.5 m.   Hardiness: 2.

'Halfdan Lem' ('The Hon. Jean-Marie de Montague' x 'Red Loderi' 1975)
Foliage: deep green, 150-200 mm long.
Flowers: bright red, funnel-shaped.
Flowers per head: 9-13.
Season: 3.   Size: 2.5 m x 2.5 m.   Hardiness: 4.

'Lem's Monarch' ('Anna' x 'Marinus Koster' 1971)
Foliage: mid green, 125-200 mm long.
Flowers: white to pale pink flushed and edged deep pink, funnel-shaped.
Flowers per head: 9-15.
Season: 3.   Size: 2.5 m x 2 m.   Hardiness: 4.

'Lem's Stormcloud' ('Burgundy' x 'Mars' 1980)
Foliage: mid green, 100-150 mm long.
Flowers: deep wine red with a white throat, funnel-shaped.
Flowers per head: 9-15.
Season: 3-4.   Size: 2 m x 2 m.   Hardiness: 5.

R. 'Lem's Cameo'

R. 'Mrs G. W. Leak'

'Loderi' grex (*R. griffithianum* x *R. fortunei* 1901)
Foliage: mid green to slightly glaucous, 150-200 mm long.
Flowers: white to mid pink depending on the cultivar, fragrant, funnel-shaped.
Flowers per head: 5-11.
Season: 3.   Size: 2.5 m x 2.5 m.   Hardiness: 4.

'Mount Everest' (*R. campanulatum* x *R. griffithianum*? 1930)
Foliage: mid green, 125-175 mm long.
Flowers: white with reddish brown spotting, slightly fragrant, funnel-shaped.
Flowers per head: 7-11.
Season: 3.   Size: 2 m x 2 m.   Hardiness: 5.

'Mrs Charles E. Pearson' ('Coombe Royal' x *R. catawbiense* 'Grandiflorum' 1909)
Foliage: deep green, 125-175 mm long.
Flowers: light pink with darker markings, funnel-shaped.
Flowers per head: 13-18.
Season: 3.   Size: 3 m x 2.5 m.   Hardiness: 4.

'Mrs G.W. Leak' ('Coombe Royal' x 'Chevalier Felix de Sauvage' before 1934)
Foliage: mid green, 100-150 mm long.
Flowers: light pink with conspicuous reddish pink throat markings, funnel-shaped.
Flowers per head: 9-12.
Season: 3.   Size: 2.5 m x 2 m.   Hardiness: 4.

R. 'Purple Splendour'

'Naomi' grex ('Aurora' x *R. fortunei* 1926)
Foliage: mid green to slightly glaucous, 125-175 mm long.
Flowers: pink and cream to apricot-pink and soft yellow (varies with the cultivar), funnel-shaped.
Flowers per head: 9-13.
Season: 3.   Size: 2 m x 1.8 m.   Hardiness: 4.

'Olin O. Dobbs ('Mars' x 'Purple Splendour' 1979)
Foliage: deep green, slightly glossy, 100-150 mm long.
Flowers: deep purplish-red, funnel-shaped.
Flowers per head: 11-15.
Season: 3.   Size: 1.8 m x 2 m.   Hardiness: 5.

'Pink Pearl' ('George Hardy' x 'Broughtonii' 1897)
Foliage: mid green, 90-125 mm long.
Flowers: deep pink buds open mid pink and fade to pale pink, funnel-shaped.
Flowers per head: 11-15.
Season: 3.   Size: 3 m x 2 m.   Hardiness: 4.

'Purple Splendour' (*ponticum* hybrid before 1900)
Foliage: dark green, narrow, slightly glossy, 75-125 mm long.
Flowers: purple with very dark throat markings, funnel-shaped.
Flowers per head: 7-14.
Season: 3-4.   Size: 2 m x 1.8 m.   Hardiness: 4.

'Sappho' (unknown before 1847)
Foliage: deep green, narrow, 100-150 mm long.
Flowers: white with blackish-purple throat markings, funnel-shaped.
Flowers per head: 5-11.
Season: 4.   Size: 2 m x 2 m.   Hardiness: 5.

'Susan' (*R. campanulatum* x *R. fortunei* 1930)
Foliage: deep green, glossy, 100-140 mm long.
Flowers: lavender blue, funnel-shaped.
Flowers per head: 5-11.
Season: 3.   Size: 2 m x 1.8 m.   Hardiness: 4.

'Trude Webster' ('Countess of Derby' selfed 1961)
Foliage: mid green, 150-200 mm long.
Flowers: clear mid pink, funnel-shaped.
Flowers per head: 15-20.
Season: 3.   Size: 2 m x 2 m.   Hardiness: 5.

'Van Nes Sensation' ('Sir Charles Butler' x 'Halopeanum')
Foliage: mid green, 125-175 mm long.
Flowers: pink buds open white suffused pink, slightly fragrant, funnel-shaped.
Flowers per head: 7-11.
Season: 3.   Size: 2 m x 1.8 m.   Hardiness: 4.

Vireya rhododendrons

The tropical vireya rhododendrons have always enjoyed a fairly limited popularity as greenhouse or frost-free garden plants. Also known as malesian or Malaysian rhododendrons, they form a separate section of seven subsections within the subgenus Rhododendron. There are around 250 species, most of which are natural epiphytes that occur in the high rainfall areas of South-East Asia through to northern Australia, with many from Borneo and New Guinea. Vireyas tend to be rather straggly 1.5 m x 1.5 m plants, but they make up for their untidy growth habit with very brightly coloured and often fragrant flowers. Most produce rather loose heads of about 3–7 blooms.

Vireyas are not difficult to grow provided they are protected from frost. Because they tend to be high altitude plants, most will tolerate prolonged exposure to relatively cool temperatures but few can withstand anything

R. 'Candy'

R. 'Simbu Sunset'

but the very lightest frosts. In most cases all that is required is a frost-free greenhouse or conservatory, but supplementary light and a little extra heat will often yield better results.

Vireyas are not strictly seasonal in their flowering and blooms are possible at any time. Flower buds are most likely to form in late summer and open in autumn or winter, which is another reason for considering additional heat in cool climates: the buds may not open properly if their development is checked by cold.

If you live in a mild frost-free climate you can treat vireyas much like any other rhododendron. The epiphytic species usually adapt well to growing in the soil provided it is free draining. In colder areas the plants are generally grown in containers; use a coarse potting mix with added humus. They should be fed occasionally with mild liquid fertilisers. If you intend to grow your vireyas in a greenhouse it may be better to create large beds rather than having the plants in individual pots. Pots tend to dry out quickly and are inclined to tip over as the plants are often very top-heavy.

Among the more common vireyas are:
R. aurigeranum: orange yellow.
'Candy': pale pink, fragrant.
R. christianae: deep golden-yellow.
R. jasminiflorum: white, fragrant, 1 m x 1 m.
R. javanicum: orange edged yellow.
R. konori: pale pink, fragrant.
R. laetum: bright yellow to orange.
R. lochae: bright red.
R. macgregoriae: golden-yellow.
'Tropic Glow': yellow edged orange.
'Simbu Sunset': yellow edged orange.
R. zoelleri: golden yellow edged orange.

Deciduous azaleas

Deciduous azalea hybrids are divided into groups based on their parentage. The main groups are as follows:

Ghent

In the early 1800s Ghent, Belgium was the main centre for azalea breeding. The earliest hybrids were raised from *R. calendulaceum*, *R. nudiflorum*, *R. luteum* and *R. viscosum*. Later, *R. molle* was crossed with *R. viscosum*

Exbury azalea 'Cannon's Double'

to produce the viscosepalum hybrids. These were popular for a while, but they have now largely disappeared. However, the later Ghent hybrids show some influence of this cross as well as *R. periclymenoides*.

Further developments include the double Ghent or rustica strain. These plants, introduced from the late 1850s, were followed in 1890 by a similar group of double-flowered hybrids known as rustica flore pleno hybrids. The parentage of these later doubles is not known for sure, but they probably result from crossing the original double Ghents with *R. japonicum*.

When Ghent hybrids were at the height of their popularity over 500 cultivars were available. Today they have been largely superseded by later styles and probably no more than 20 cultivars are commonly grown.

They tend to be large (around 2 m x 2 m), late-flowering plants that are all hardy to -20°C. Although the flowers are relatively small (about 50 mm in diameter), they are carried in large heads and are often fragrant.

Ghents are not common but you may see:
'Coccinea Speciosa': bright orange-red.
'Daviesii': white, fragrant.
'Narcissiflora': light yellow, double, fragrant.
'Phoebe': deep yellow, double.
'Vulcan': deep red with an orange blotch.

Mollis

The mollis azaleas were developed in Belgium and the Netherlands from the Ghent azaleas. They show a greater *R. japonicum (molle)* influence than the Ghents and some of them may actually be forms of *R. japonicum (molle)* rather than hybrids. The first mollis hybrids started to appear in the late 1860s and were further refined over the next 30 years.

Because mollis azaleas can be difficult to propagate by cuttings, this group includes a number of seedling strains. These reproduce reasonably true to type, but it is best to choose your plants when in flower as any label description is likely to be only an approximation.

Mollis azaleas flower from mid spring and are usually large plants — around 2 m x 2 m. Bright yellow, orange and red are the predominant colours. The flowers are larger than the Ghents and they are all singles. Mollis azaleas are all hardy to at least -15°C and many will tolerate -20°C or lower.

Although mollis hybrids have declined in popularity in recent years, the following hybrids are still commonly available:

'Anthony Koster': bright yellow with an orange blotch.

'Apple Blossom': light pink.

'Christopher Wren': bright yellow with an orange blotch.

'Dr M. Oosthoek': reddish-orange.

'Floradora': bright orange.

'J.C. van Tol': apricot pink.

'Orange Glow': apricot with an orange blotch.

'Winston Churchill': orange-red.

Occidentale

Rhododendron occidentale is a fragrant white- to pink-flowered deciduous azalea from the west coast of the United States. It was discovered in 1827 and entered cultivation in the 1850s.

Occidentale hybrids are among the most fragrant azaleas and usually develop into large plants (around 2.5 m x 2.5 m), although they are quite slow-growing. They bloom from mid spring and have flowers up to 80 mm in diameter. White and pale pink are the predominant colours, but most culti-

Ilam azalea 'Louie Williams'

vars have very conspicuous golden throat markings.

The most common occidentale hybrids are:

'Delicatissima': creamy white, flushed pink.

'Exquisita': white flushed pink.

'Graciosa': pale apricot to orange.

'Irene Koster': white flushed dark pink.

Knap Hill, Exbury & Ilam

The Knap Hill, Exbury and Ilam azaleas are the most widely grown deciduous hybrids. The original plants were developed from about 1870 at the Knap Hill, England, nursery of Anthony Waterer. Starting with Ghent azaleas, he crossbred extensively and selected only the best of the resultant hybrids. Waterer named only one of his plants, 'Nancy Waterer', and it was not until the seedlings were acquired by Sunningdale Nurseries on the death of Waterer's son in 1924 that plants began to be made available to the public.

Lionel de Rothschild of Exbury obtained several Knap Hill seedlings in 1922 and from these developed the Exbury strain. The first of these, 'Hotspur', was introduced in 1934. The collection was almost lost during World War Two and relatively few hybrids were introduced until the 1950s.

Exbury azalea 'Gibraltar'

Edgar Stead of Ilam, in Christchurch, New Zealand, working with various species and Ghent and Knap Hill hybrids, further refined the strain. Stead's work was continued by Dr J.S. Yeates until his recent death. His Melford strain includes some of the best deciduous hybrids.

These azaleas are usually large plants (about 2m x 2m) that flower from mid spring. Intense yellow, orange and red shades predominate, but there are also bright pink and cultivars in pastel shades.

There are hundreds of Knap Hill, Exbury and Ilam azaleas and they are the most widely available of the deciduous hybrids. Some of the best are:

'Brazil': orange red.
'Cannon's Double': light yellow, double, low-growing.
'Carmen': apricot with orange markings.
'Cecile': red with yellow markings.
'Chaffinch': deep pink.
'Gallipoli': apricot with orange markings.
'Gibraltar': orange red.
'Homebush': purplish-red, semi-double.
'Hotspur': reddish-orange.
'Louie Williams': light pink and soft yellow.
'Maori': bright orange red.
'Ming': orange and yellow.
'Persil': white with a yellow blotch.
'Pink Delight': bright pink with a golden-yellow throat.
'Yellow Giant': bright yellow.

Some of these forms are available as seedling strains but these are slowly being replaced by cutting-grown plants.

Other groups

Many hybridisers have raised deciduous azaleas. In general they do not vary greatly from the main groups. Most have been developed in the United States and have only localised distribution. The Girard and Carlson hybrids are probably the most important of these lesser-known groups.

Evergreen azaleas

Evergreen azaleas are divided into groups based on their parentage. The following is a very brief outline of the main groups.

Indica

The first indica hybrids were developed in Belgium in the 1850s and were intended to be used as house plants. These hybrids have *Rhododendron simsii*, a native of South-East Asia, in their breeding. This species is only hardy to about -4°C so it is not surprising that this group includes some frost-tender hybrids.

R. simsii was used because it produces bi-colour flowers and can easily be forced into bloom in the winter. These forced plants are frequently sold as 'house azaleas'. They are no different from the cultivars grown in gardens except that they may have been artificially dwarfed.

There are several indica azalea sub groups, the most important of which are the Belgian, Kerrigan and Rutherford indicas. These are very similar to one another and simply represent various breeders' efforts along the same lines.

Indicas are the fanciest azaleas with an

enormous range of frilly doubles and multi-colour flowers. They are the plants that, when in flower, many nurseries use for promotions and counter displays. If your climate is mild enough to grow them, they are no more difficult than any other azalea, but remember that most indicas will be badly damaged if regularly exposed to frosts of -6°C or lower.

There are thousands of indica hybrids, of which hundreds are regularly available. Also, new plants are always being introduced. There is a lot of duplication among these hybrids. Some of the most distinctive are:

'Albert Elizabeth'
Flowers: white with a reddish-pink edge, semi-double.
Season: 1-2.　Size: 50 cm x 75 cm.　Hardiness: 1.

'Bride Bouquet'
Flowers: white, double.
Season: 3.　Size: 70 cm x 1 m.　Hardiness: 2.

'Comptesse de Kerchove'
Flowers: apricot pink, double.
Season: 1-3.　Size: 50 cm x 75 cm.　Hardiness: 2.

'De Waele's Favourite'
Flowers: white edged and marked deep pink, double.
Season: 2-3.　Size: 50 cm x 75 m.　Hardiness: 2.

Kerrigan Indica 'Bride's Bouquet'

Belgian Indica 'Red Wings'

'Fielder's White'
Flowers: white, single, slightly fragrant.
Season: 2-3.
Size: 1.5 m x 1.8 m.　Hardiness: 2.

'Glory of Sunninghill'
Flowers: intense cerise, single.
Season: 4-5.　Size: 1 m x 1.5 m.　Hardiness: 2.

'Goyet'
Flowers: deep red, semi-double.
Season: 3.　Size: 80 cm x 1 m.　Hardiness: 2.

'James Belton'
Flowers: very pale pink, single.
Season: 2.　Size: 50 cm x 1 m.　Hardiness: 2.

'Orchid Gem'
Flowers: purple, single.
Season: 2-3.　Size: 1.5 cm x 1.5 m.　Hardiness: 2.

'Red Wings'
Flowers: Deep pinkish-red, single to hose in hose.
Season: 2-3.　Size: 50 cm x 1 m.　Hardiness: 2.

'Ripples'
Flowers: deep cerise, double.
Season: 2-3.　Size: 60 cm x 1 m.　Hardiness: 2.

'Rose Queen'
Flowers: pale pink flushed deep pink, hose in hose.
Season: 1-3.　Size: 50 cm x 1 m.　Hardiness: 2.

Belgian Indica 'Southern Aurora'

'Southern Aurora'
Flowers: white edged and suffused orange,
double.
Season: 1-3.   Size: 50 cm x 75 cm.   Hardiness: 2.

'Violacea'
Flowers: purple, semi-double.
Season: 1-3.   Size: 50 cm x 1 m.   Hardiness: 2.

Kurume

Kurume, a town in Kyushu, the southern-most main island of Japan, has for many years been a major azalea-growing area. In 1919 the famous plant collector Ernest 'Chinese' Wilson visited Kurume and bought examples of 50 cultivars, which he introduced to Western gardens as 'Wilson's fifty'. Since then many further hybrids have been raised and introduced.

Kurume azaleas clearly show the influence of *Rhododendron kiusianum*, a species that grows wild on Mt Kirishima. They are dense compact growers with small leaves and masses of small flowers early in the season. Many Kurume azaleas, such as the very popular 'Kirin', have hose in hose flowers. This is a style of bloom in which the sepals become petal-like and create the effect of a second corolla.

With great age these azaleas can become large plants, but they may be kept trimmed to about 80 cm x 1 m if necessary. Most are hardy to about -12 to -15°C.

'Addy Wery': deep orange red, single.
'Cherry Blossom': white flushed red, hose in hose.
'Christmas Cheer': intense cerise, single to hose in hose.
'Hino Crimson': intense cerise, single.
'Kirin': mid pink, hose in hose.
'Kocho No Mai': purple, single.
'Orange Beauty': orange-red, single.
'Osaraku': white suffused lavender, single.
'Red Robin': vivid orange-red, single.
'Ward's Ruby': deep red.

Kaempferi

This group includes the hardiest evergreen azalea hybrids. They are derived from *Rhododendron kaempferi* and *Rhododendron yedoense*, both of which will withstand -20°C, although when exposed to very low temperatures they will drop most of their foliage.

Most Kaempferi hybrids originate from the United States and the Netherlands. They have, until recently, been bred primarily for hardiness but many of the newer hybrids

Kurume azalea 'Kirin'

have quite fancy flowers. Kaempferis often develop red foliage tints in winter.

They vary in their flowering season but most bloom mid spring. They tend to have large flowers with relatively few full double or hose in hose flowered cultivars. They often make up for their lack of flower complexity with extremely intense colours.

Kaempferis vary in size but most are ultimately large plants. The average size is 1.2 m x 1.5 m at 10 years old.

'Blue Danube': purple, hose in hose, frilled.

'Double Beauty': deep pink, hose in hose.

'Florida': deep pink, hose in hose.

'Girard's Border Gem': deep cerise-pink, single, 60 cm x 80 cm.

'Johanna': deep red, single to semi-double.

'Lorna': deep pink, hose in hose double.

'Vuyk's Scarlet': red, single to semi-double.

Satsuki

Most gardeners regard the Kurume azaleas as the traditional Japanese azalea, while the Japanese regard the Satsuki as the more typical azalea. The confusion is probably because Kurumes have been in cultivation in Western gardens for longer than the Satsukis; as the latter have only been widely grown since the 1950s.

Satsuki means fifth month. This is not a direct reference to May in the Northern Hemisphere but it does give an indication of the flowering time. Satsukis flower late, some very late, so they need protection from the summer sun if their flowers are to last.

Satsukis are usually hardy to about -12°C. They have large single flowers with highly variable colouration. One plant can display a wide range of colour and pattern. This puts some gardeners off but others feel that it gives the plants more individuality.

Most Satsukis are small spreading bushes. Some hybrids may be up to 1 m x 1.5 m but most are around 50 cm x 1 m. The very dwarf Gumpo Satsukis are often used in rockeries.

Satsuki azalea 'Hitoya No Haru'

'Benigasa': deep orange red.

'Chinzan': deep reddish-pink, 30 cm x 60 cm.

'Gumpo': a group of 30 cm x 60 cm hybrids that are available in various shades of pink, lavender and white.

'Gunrei': white flushed and striped mid pink.

'Hitoya No Haru': lavender pink.

'Issho No Haru': pale pink.

'Shiko': light purple.

'Shugetsu': white edged purple.

Inter-group

This is a catch-all group that includes hybrids produced by breeding between the other groups as well as those raised from newly introduced species. Obviously this is a wide-ranging group and includes all manner of sizes, flower types and degrees of hardiness. Among the best inter-group hybrids are:

'Bayou'
Flowers: very pale pink, semi-double.
Season: 3.   Size: 50 cm x 1 m.   Hardiness: 2.

Glenn Dale Inter-Group 'Ben Morrison'

'Ben Morrison'
Flowers: rusty red with a white border, single.
Season: 3.   Size: 1.5 m x 1.8 m.   Hardiness: 3.

'Betty-Ann Voss'
Flowers: mid pink, semi-double.
Season: 4.   Size: 50 cm x 1 m.   Hardiness: 3.

'Fascination'
Flowers: red with a pale pink or white centre, single.
Season: 4.   Size: 50 cm x 70 cm.   Hardiness: 2.

'Festive'
Flowers: white with mauve flecks, single.
Season: 2.   Size: 1.5 m x 1.5 m.   Hardiness: 4.

'Glacier'
Flowers: white, single.
Season: 3.   Size: 1.5 m x 1.8 m.   Hardiness: 4.

'Great Expectations'
Flowers: orange-red, double.
Season: 4-5.   Size: 50 cm x 1.2 m.   Hardiness: 4.

'Happy Days'
Flowers: purple, double.
Season: 2.   Size: 75 cm x 1 m.   Hardiness: 2.

'Lady Louise'
Flowers: deep apricot pink, semi-double.
Season: 3.   Size: 70 cm x 1 m.   Hardiness: 4.

'Martha Hitchcock'
Flowers: white with a mauve border, single.
Season: 3-4.
Size: 1.5 m x 1.8 m.   Hardiness: 4.

'Miss Suzie'
Flowers: bright red, hose in hose.
Season: 3.   Size: 60 cm x 80 cm.   Hardiness: 3.

'Pearl Bradford Sport'
Flowers: deep purplish-pink, single.
Season: 5.   Size: 30 cm x 50 cm.   Hardiness: 4.

'Pink Pancake'
Flowers: salmon pink, single.
Season: 4-5.   Size: 20 cm x 1.2 cm.   Hardiness: 4.

'Susannah Hill'
Flowers: red, single.
Season: 4-5.   Size: 30 cm x 1.2 m.   Hardiness: 4.

'Tenino'
Flowers: light purple, single.
Season: 3-4.   Size: 30 cm x 75 cm.   Hardiness: 4.

'White Rosebud'
Flowers: white, double.
Season: 4.   Size: 80 cm x 1 m.   Hardiness: 4.

Glenn Dale Inter-Group 'Festive'

Chapter 7
PLANTING AND MAINTENANCE

Satsuki azalea 'Chinzan'

HAVING carefully selected a rhododendron and bought it, you now need to plant it.

Assuming that you have taken the time to work in plenty of compost before planting, the drainage should be reasonably good but check it just to make sure. Dig a 50-cm deep hole and fill it with water. If the water has drained within about 4–6 hours the drainage should be adequate. If the hole fills with water as you dig then you have a high water table and will need to improve the drainage or plant in raised beds.

It is very common for rhododendrons to grow well until they are about five or six years old, then suddenly start to drop foliage, become yellow and die back. This can nearly always be traced back to root rots caused by poor drainage. The plants are fine until their roots hit the subsoil clay or they begin to enter the level of the permanent water table. When that happens, the roots can no longer spread to find nutrients and the plant begins to suffer through a lack of root devel-

opment and gradual starvation.

Regular feeding will help affected plants recover, but prevention is always better than cure: the answer is a well-drained site and extra preparation. This is especially so with large plants. It is all very well preparing the top 50 cm of soil for a 1.5 m high plant, but larger plants have larger root systems that go down deeper than that. Although rhododendrons are very shallow rooted compared to most plants, a tree-sized specimen will still be anchored by a substantial root system.

Good drainage needs to be taken care of at planting time. The very least you can do is to work in compost and drainage material to a depth of 80 cm–1 m. Planting on raised ground is also a good idea. This can be a naturally higher part of the garden or an artificial mound. If poor drainage is still a possibility or you have a very hard clay-pan, field drains may need to be laid. These should drain the soil to at least a depth of 1 m. If you can go deeper, so much the better.

Evergreen azaleas, like all rhododendrons, require good drainage.

It is also a good idea to incorporate a mild general fertiliser prior to planting. Fresh animal manures and harsh chemical fertilisers can burn tender young roots so stick to mild fertilisers. Make sure they are well worked into the soil.

Only when you are satisfied that the ground is thoroughly prepared is it time to plant. Newly planted rhododendrons need loose soil in order to make quick root growth, so make sure you dig a hole that is at least twice the size of the plant's root ball.

Thoroughly soak the shrub before you remove it from its container or the roots may adhere to the sides and suffer damage. Plastic bags may be cut away or carefully eased off and most rhododendrons in hard pots come away cleanly if the pot is upended and given a firm rap on the rim. If the shrub appears pot bound, gently loosen up the root ball. Otherwise just lightly work your fingers into the root ball to allow moisture to penetrate and spread out a few of the lower roots to get them growing in the right direction.

Place the rhododendron in the hole and check the soil level. Plant with the soil at the same level as it was in the container. Gently firm the plant into position with your heel as you replace the soil, but don't ram the soil back into place or you will undo all the work that went into loosening it up.

Mulch around the plant and stake large rhododendrons to prevent wind-rock. In dry areas or on sloping sites it is a good idea to make a rim of soil or mulch around new plants to act as a reservoir that can be filled when the plants are watered.

Watering

Water well during the first summer but don't drown the young plants. Make sure the root ball is thoroughly soaked. Plants raised in potting mix, as most rhododendrons now are, can be very difficult to re-wet once they have dried out. It is very easy to think you are watering well when all that is happening is that the soil around the plant is getting wet while the all-important root ball remains dry.

If the plant is slow to come into growth despite watering and feeding, it may be that the root ball is still dry at the centre. The only way to check this is to probe around the roots. If the roots closest to the main stem are not noticeably dry, you may have to lift the plant to check the roots. This will also highlight any problems with root-feeding insects or root rots.

Weeding and mulching

Young plants are easily smothered by weeds and older plants may suffer if they have to compete with large weeds, so weed control is essential. Rhododendrons are easily damaged by chemical sprays and hoeing because their feeding roots are very close to the surface. Pulling weeds by hand or levering them out with a small hand fork is the safest method. Mulching will prevent many weeds becoming established and makes those that do grow easier to remove.

Mulching with compost or material such as rotted pine bark in spring will also help to conserve moisture and will insulate the surface roots from hot sun during the summer. An autumn mulch will prevent the soil becoming compacted by winter rains and lessen the effect of frosts on the surface roots.

Compost, rotted sawdust, rotted straw and bark chips are all good mulching materials. Spent potting mix also makes a good mulch. Very light materials, such as peat, tend to be blown away and grass clippings get too hot unless they are thoroughly composted first. A mixture of fine and medium grade bark chips is attractive and functional. The larger pieces rise to the surface and prevent the fine, moisture-holding bark from blowing away.

Leaf gall on azalea 'Silver Glow'.

Avoid mounding mulch up against the trunk or main stems of larger rhododendrons it may cause a deterioration in the bark and lead to fungal or viral troubles.

Diseases

Grown under good conditions, rhododendrons are relatively free of diseases. You may encounter common fungal diseases such as botrytis, galls, rust and powdery mildew but these are quite easily controlled with good ventilation, good plant hygiene and common fungicides.

Root rot diseases, especially root rot (caused by the fungus *Phytophthora cinnamomi*) can sometimes be a problem, particularly in poorly drained soil. There is little you can do to control these diseases, but making sure the plants are not too crowded and that the drainage is satisfactory will go a long way to preventing them occurring in the first place. Soil fungicides can be used to prevent root rot but it is difficult to know where the disease is going to strike. In most cases only one or two plants are affected, so it is something that can be tolerated.

Phytophthora syringae is a closely related fungus that causes a dieback effect on the branches. It is a relatively recent discovery that is not yet widespread. *Phomopsis* dieback is a more common disease that mainly affects azaleas. It causes twigs and branches

Some rhododendrons, particularly Loderis like 'King George', pictured here, are prone to viral infections that cause leaf spotting.

to die back and may eventually prove fatal, although this usually takes several years. If odd branches show signs of wilting and yellow foliage yet there is no sign of frost damage, suspect *Phomopsis* dieback. The disease can be controlled by removing any affected branches and spraying with a fungicide. Organically acceptable copper and sulphur sprays work reasonably well but systemic sprays provide better control.

Pestalotia fungi cause sunburn-like markings of the foliage, particularly around the leaf tip and along the margins. Although clearly not sunburn, which usually scorches the centre of the leaf, this disease can be difficult to differentiate from fertiliser burn as this causes very similar leaf tip browning. If no fertiliser has been used, you should suspect pestalotia. Many fungicides will control this problem and good ventilation goes a long way towards peventing it.

Azalea leaf gall is a fungal disease that attacks the new growth and the flowers. It causes an unsightly thickening and distorting of foliage and petals and can spread quickly in cool, moist weather. Picking off affected leaves and petals and spraying with a suitable fungicide, such as mancozeb, will control the disease. This is mainly a cosmetic problem that causes little long-term damage.

Bud blast or bud blight is a fungal disease that attacks unopened buds, causing them to turn brown and fail to open. It would be difficult to distinguish from frost damage were it not for the fine black filaments (coremia) that develop on the buds. Infected buds should be removed and destroyed and the plant treated with a fungicide. Copper-based sprays are effective. Bud blight may occasionally spread to the branches.

Ovulinia petal blight is a disease that destroys the flowers as they open. It starts as 1 mm-diameter spots that look brown and watery and gradually the whole flower becomes a slimy light brown mess. This fungal disease can spread quickly in the cool moist weather that is common in spring. Good ventilation will help to control it but spraying with a fungicide is usually also necessary. The disease spores winter over in the soil, so the soil should be drenched with a fungicide during winter in areas where outbreaks are known to occur.

Many rhododendrons develop purple leaf spots in winter. These are not signs of a disease but appear to be related to stress from the cold weather. Leaves that roll along the midrib and curl down are also common in cold weather.

Ring-like purple spotting on the foliage is common with *R. griffithianum* hybrids such as those of the Loderi grex. Although this is a sign of a viral infection that can cause premature leaf drop, it is seldom a serious problem. In any case, the disease is virtually impossible to eradicate and is something you have to live with if you wish to grow the otherwise superb hybrids.

Pests

Few of the pests that attack rhododendrons are life threatening and provided you are prepared to put up with a few chewed leaves little in the way of control is required.

Caterpillars, especially leaf-roller caterpillars, looper caterpillars, and cutworms all

The subterranean larvae of this weevil can cause serious damage to potted plants by destroying the roots. The adult (pictured) is usually nocturnal and damages the foliage by chewing its edges.

cause damage by chewing the foliage and occasionally the buds and flowers. Most can be removed by hand or controlled with safe insecticides.

Azalea leaf miners can cause significant damage by destroying the foliage and retarding growth. The small caterpillars, which are common on evergreen azaleas, start life within the leaf and feed by burrowing (mining) between the upper and lower surfaces of the leaf. Later, when they become too large to remain within the leaf, they emerge and make a shelter by rolling over the tip of the leaf. Because these insects are inside the leaf, systemic insecticides are the only truly effective control.

Thrips, lace bugs and spider mites may all be found on the underside of rhododendron leaves. They can cause severe damage by rasping the foliage and sucking the sap. Their presence is usually indicated by leaves that develop silver-grey upper surfaces. An examination of the undersurface will reveal a sticky brown honeydew deposit, which can lead to the development of sooty mould diseases. Oil sprays and other safe insecticides can control these pests but it is very important to get complete coverage.

Damage from root-feeding weevil and bee-tle larvae can be a serious problem with container-grown plants. In the garden these pests are seldom present in sufficient numbers to cause great damage, however, in a container they can quickly kill a plant by eating away most of the roots. Occasionally sprinkling the soil surface of container plants with a soil insecticide will prevent such potential disasters. Rhododendron weevils will also chew the foliage, but if the larvae are controlled than adults are rarely a serious problem. The weevils feed at night and may be removed by hand.

Pruning

Rhododendrons do not need regular pruning but they do occasionally need to be trimmed, and a lot of later work can be avoided if plants are trained into a good shape when young.

Dead-heading, which is the removal of old flowers and seed heads, is an important part of the shaping process. Removing the seed heads allows the plant to channel its energies into growth rather than seed production. Check the shape of the plant while dead-heading; remove any crowded, weak or diseased branches close to the main stem, and pinch out the apical leaf-bud from any non-flowering stems. This will produce an evenly shaped bush and encourage strong lateral branching and dense growth.

Sometimes you will need to go a little further. Although there is no complicated science involved in trimming rhododendrons, there are a few points that ought to be considered.

Any trimming and shaping is best done immediately after flowering because this allows the whole growing season for regrowth and lessens the effect of pruning on the following season's flowering. The flower buds form in the late summer and autumn so any pruning done after early summer will limit the amount of bud-bearing regrowth that can develop before the buds are initiated.

Kurume azalea 'Red Robin' always has masses of flowers and can be relied upon to make a vivid display.

Start by thinning out the centre of the bush to improve the ventilation. Cut back any spindly or diseased branches and remove any congested growth. Now you can start to shape the bush. This is just a matter of cutting back any overly long branches and evening up the growth. Always cut elepidote rhododendrons back to a whorl of leaves because that is where the most vigorous buds are located.

Azaleas and lepidote rhododendrons have slightly different pruning requirements. They will usually reshoot from anywhere on the plant and can be sheared to shape. Compact, small-leafed azaleas are ideal subjects for hedging and topiary. More precise shaping is possible, but it is seldom necessary to do anything more than head back any extra vigorous growth and remove damaged or weak wood.

Unlike other deciduous plants, deciduous azaleas should not be pruned during the winter or the flower buds will be removed. Remove any weak stems immediately after flowering and cut the bush back to four or five main branches. You can be quite severe as the bush will quickly recover. The new growth that develops will often be very vigorous and should be pinched back before it gets too long. This will encourage lateral branching and helps to produce strong healthy branches rather than the spindly twigs often seen on deciduous azaleas.

Very old, overgrown plants can be cut back to stumps, but heavy pruning should be done with care because rhododendrons are sometimes reluctant to reshoot from bare wood. Although a well-established plant will generally reshoot from a bare stump provided it is healthy, it is often better to prune in

83

easier stages over two seasons. Hard-pruned plants can take several years before resuming normal flowering, and further shaping is often required as the growth develops.

Careful attention to shaping and dead-heading will result in healthier, more compact plants that flower heavily.

Feeding

Rhododendrons are not heavy feeders. Most of their needs can be met by incorporating a general acid plant food with the mulch when it is applied. Slow-release fertiliser granules are also an effective feeding method. Mild liquid fertilisers can be applied during the growing season.

Any fertilisers should be well diluted or watered in because it is very easy to burn the surface roots. This will result in leaf scorching in mild cases, while very strong fertiliser doses may kill the young foliage.

Fertilisers can be used throughout the growing season but you should cease feeding at the end of summer or you may find that the plants are still in soft growth when the first frosts occur. Commercial growers often apply sulphate of potash in the autumn as this helps to ensure that the wood ripens properly. This is important for commercial growers as they tend to keep feeding their plants well into autumn in order to get the maximum growth out of them, but it is unnecessary for most home gardeners provided a natural autumn ripening period is allowed for.

Transplanting

Because rhododendrons have compact, shallow root systems with few heavy roots, they are very easily transplanted at almost any time of the year. There is no restriction on the size of plant that can be transplanted, other than your ability to lift it.

The first step is to prepare a hole at the destination. Dig a hole to what you think will be roughly the depth of the plant's roots, then increase the diameter and depth of the hole working in compost as you dig. You will regret not doing this first if you lift the plant and then find some unforeseen complication at the new planting site.

When you have the site thoroughly prepared you can lift the rhododendron. Dig around the plant well away from the main stem and take as large a root ball as you can manage. You should find that with even a large rhododendron most of its roots are in the top 50 cm of soil.

The next step, lifting the plant, is fraught with difficulties. Under-estimating the weight of a mature rhododendron and its ball of roots is a sure way to damage your back. Sometimes the plant can be slid onto a sack or tarpaulin and dragged to its destination or you may be able manoeuvre a wheelbarrow under the shrub, but often you will need assistance to hoist the plant onto a barrow or trolley.

Before replanting, check that the hole is about the right depth — you don't want to have to lift the plant again if you can avoid it. Nevertheless it is not uncommon to have to remove a little more soil or to put some back. When the plant is in the right position, refill the hole, making sure you eliminate any air pockets under the root ball. Other than the usual staking, mulching and watering, little in the way of aftercare is required. Most rhododendrons carry on growing apparently unchecked and can even be moved in flower.

Chapter 8

PROPAGATION

Azalea 'Greenwood Orange'

ALTHOUGH it is possible to buy a wide range of species and cultivars as ready-grown plants, most enthusiasts eventually start to propagate their own rhododendrons. They are not, however, always the easiest plants to propagate.

All rhododendrons may be raised from seed and it is a reasonably straightforward process, but seedlings may take several years to reach flowering age and cultivars will not reproduce true to type from seed. Unless you are only interested in propagating species you will also need to be able to raise plants vegetatively.

The most common vegetative method is the cutting. By removing a small piece of stem from the parent plant, placing it in a suitable growing medium and keeping it under controlled conditions, it can be induced to form roots and may then be grown on as a new plant.

Other common vegetative techniques include layering, aerial layering and grafting.

Although the methods vary depending on the type of rhododendron being propagated, cuttings are by far the most common.

Seed

As mentioned above, growing from seed is not a practical method for cultivars and selected varieties as they do not reproduce true to type. Some deciduous azaleas, however, are difficult to propagate by other means and have, over the years, been bred to the point where it is possible to raise reliably true colour strains from seed. These are sometimes sold as named varieties but they generally just go by a colour name.

Growing rhododendrons from seed is not difficult but there may be a considerable waiting period before you see any flowers. This varies from about 18 months for some of the evergreen azaleas to more than five years for most of the larger rhododendrons. Tree-sized rhododendrons may not flower until they are more than 10 years old.

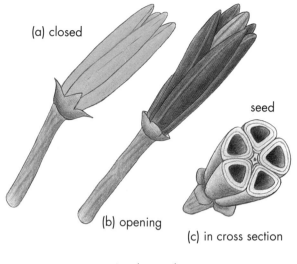

(a) closed

(b) opening

seed

(c) in cross section

Seed capsule

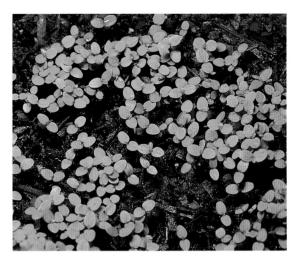

Rhododendron seedlings are very small, but they are tough and easy to care for.

Seed may be bought, produced by hybridising, or collected from plants that have been naturally pollinated.

Seed houses that specialise in shrubs and trees usually stock a wide range of rhododendron species and many rhododendron societies will supply seed to their members. When you buy rhododendron species seed you will find that some types are numbered. These collectors' numbers refer to the original specimen collected in the wild. They are a useful way of identifying local variations in a species but are not of great significance for the beginner.

When harvesting seed it can be difficult to determine if the seed pods are ripe. You do not want the seed to be immature but you cannot leave it too late or the pods will burst and scatter the seed. The only answer to this is experience. Often there will be colour changes or drying as the seed pod nears maturity, but you may have to harvest slightly unripe pods and ripen them indoors to avoid losing the seed. Sometimes it is possible to catch falling seed by tying a small paper bag over the ripening pods.

Sow your seed on a finely sieved 50/50 mixture of sphagnum moss and peat- or bark-based potting mix. Do not cover the seed, just sow it on the surface and gently moisten it with a fine mist. If it is kept lightly shaded and moist it should germinate in about ten days to six weeks depending on the type. The seed keeps reasonably well but the highest germination percentages are attained by sowing immediately after harvest, which is usually in the autumn. However, unless you can provide artificial light and heat, delay sowing (especially deciduous azaleas) until spring because without added light and warmth autumn-germinated seed-lings will often collapse over winter.

Rhododendron seed is usually very fine and the young seedlings are minute and slow growing. To achieve the best results they really must be grown under conditions where you control the environment; they are generally not suitable for sowing outdoors either in trays or the open ground. The young seedlings do best with high humidity, steady, even warmth (around 18°C) and occasional dilute liquid feeding.

The seedlings can be potted on once they have formed their first true leaves, although they may still be too small to handle conveniently at this stage. No harm will come to them if they are left in the seed tray until they are easier to handle provided their nu-

Cuttings before and after preparation.

trient requirements are met. Rhododendron seedlings normally transplant well and establish quickly.

Cuttings

All rhododendrons, including the deciduous azaleas, are propagated by softwood or semiripe cuttings. A mist propagating unit with bottom heat is highly recommended, although you will be able to achieve reasonable success using pots or cutting trays enclosed in plastic tents. It is vital that the cutting environment is humid because any wilting will cause stress that the cuttings may not recover from.

Softwood cuttings are taken from the new growth before it has started to harden off and usually before it is fully expanded. They strike and develop quickly because they are taken from the most actively growing part of the plant where cell division is occurring most quickly. However, softwood cuttings are easily damaged and prone to wilting under the slightest moisture stress. Commercial growers, who have sophisticated propagating equipment, generally prefer softwood cuttings, but home gardeners, who usually operate under more primitive conditions, have more success with semi-ripe cuttings.

A semi-ripe cutting is simply a softwood cutting that has matured slightly. Its foliage

(apart from the extreme tip) will normally be fully expanded and the stem will be firm yet pliable. Semi-ripe cuttings are usually available from late spring until mid autumn.

Tip cuttings strike best. They should be three to five internodes (the space between two leaves) long plus the growing tip. The size of the cutting varies with the plant being propagated and the stage of growth. Softwood cuttings are seldom more than 100 mm long, while semi-ripe cuttings tend to be larger, typically around 150 mm, because the internodal length increases as the growth matures and expands.

Very small softwood cuttings, such as those of evergreen azaleas, can simply be snapped off at the base. Larger softwood and semi-ripe cuttings are removed with secateurs and will usually strike best if cut at a node.

Carefully strip the leaves from the lower nodes. The softer the cutting, the more likely it is to be damaged as the leaves are removed. Most leaves come away cleanly if they are removed with a quick upward pulling action after being pulled downwards just enough to break the join between the leaf and the stem.

If the leaves of the cutting are very large, it may be necessary to trim them back in order to cut down the moisture loss through transpiration and to enable more cuttings to fit in the pot or tray. The foliage can be cut back by about half but you must strike a balance between reducing transpiration loss and reducing the cuttings' ability to photosynthesise.

Before inserting a cutting into the propagating mixture dip it in a root-forming hormone. These are available in liquid, gel or powder form and can be varied in strength to suit the type of cutting. I find the semiripe strength is suitable for most cuttings.

I prefer a propagating soil made from a finely sieved 50/50 mixture of perlite and bark-based potting mix, but any well-aerated mixture using perlite, pumice, coarse river sand, potting mix or peat should be capable of producing good results. Very soft cuttings may need to be dibbled into place to stop them being bruised, but most cuttings will not be damaged if they are gently pushed into place. The cuttings can be spaced so that they are just touching, but if they are going under mist they should not overlap because leaves that are hidden under other foliage will not receive any mist.

Wounding

Because some rhododendrons are slow to strike roots, it is a common practice to wound the base of the cuttings. This involves removing a small strip of bark by making a shallow downward cut with a sharp knife or secateurs' blade along the side of the cutting immediately above the base. Wounding exposes a greater area of cambium, which can speed up the rooting process and may also produce a better root structure. It is generally restricted to the shrubby large-leafed rhododendrons and is seldom used with small-leafed rhododendrons or azaleas.

Wounding

cutting showing wound

Cutting methods

Although all rhododendrons may be grown from softwood or semi-ripe cuttings, the techniques and timing vary slightly with the style of growth.

Evergreen azaleas and small-leafed alpine rhododendrons

These plants strike best from softwood cuttings taken as soon the new spring growth is firm enough to handle, which may in some cases mean taking very small cuttings. You may continue to take cuttings right through until early autumn but those taken after early summer will not be as vigorous as the spring material, nor will they be as well established by winter. The early cuttings will strike in about six to eight weeks under mist but may take up to 12 weeks or more without mist.

Broad-leafed rhododendrons

Take semi-ripe cuttings from early summer through to mid autumn. Unless you have a misting system it may be difficult to stop early cuttings wilting. When taking cuttings after mid summer remember that you will be removing a significant number of flower buds. Flower buds should be removed before the cuttings are inserted as they are an unwanted drain on the cuttings' limited resources.

Early cuttings may strike before winter but later cuttings will probably not get under way before the following spring. Mist and bottom heat will greatly accelerate root formation and increase the strike rate.

Deciduous azaleas

Some deciduous azaleas, such as true mollis hybrids, are difficult to grow from cuttings. These varieties are usually grown from seed; modern strains produce fairly consistent results. Others, particularly the *R. occidentale* hybrids, strike easily. Take firm soft to semi-ripe cuttings from mid to late spring.

Deciduous azalea cuttings must be well struck before winter or they may collapse before spring. This can pose difficulties for those without misting systems, in which case layering or aerial layering may be better alternatives.

Layering

Layering is a good way to propagate rhododendrons that are difficult to strike from cuttings, but it is a slow process and may take up to two years to produce results.

Most rhododendrons are easily propagated by layering. Low-growing forms, particularly evergreen azaleas, will self layer where their stems touch the ground. These natural layers may be removed and grown on.

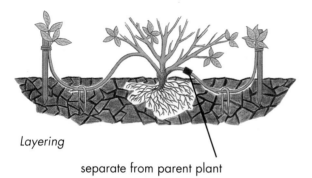

Layering

separate from parent plant

You can simulate this natural process by keeping a stem in contact with the soil, and with time roots will form. Start by selecting a pliable stem that is close to the ground. Bend it down to see if it is long enough. If it is, make a shallow cut on the lower side of the stem at the point where the soil will cover it. Dust the wound with a little rooting hormone powder, then peg the stem to the ground with a wire hoop and stake the growing tip to straighten its growth. Mound soil over the stem or if possible dig out a small trench before pegging it down, as mounded soil may blow away.

Aerial layering

You will often find that a rhododendron has no stems that can be bent down to the ground for layering. Such bushes may be propagated by aerial layering, which effectively takes the soil to the stem rather than the stem to the soil. It is also a good method for use with very large-leafed species, such as *R. sinogrande*, which make unwieldy cuttings.

Start by selecting a length of firm stem that still has green bark. Older wood will strike but it takes longer. Aerial layering can be done any time such material is available. Remove the foliage from around the immediate area and make a shallow upward cut into the stem. Lift the flap of bark and wedge it open with a matchstick or a small pebble. Lightly dust the wound with root-forming hormone powder and wrap the stem with wet sphagnum moss. Then wrap the ball of sphagnum in black polythene and secure it with wire ties or tape.

The moss will keep the wound from drying out and healing over, just like the soil in a conventional layer and with time roots will form at the wound. The layer will take a considerable time to strike; check it after about 10–12 months. When it is apparent that a good root system has formed, the layer, complete with the sphagnum, may be removed and potted up for growing on.

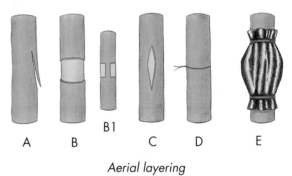

Aerial layering

A, B, B1, C and D show various methods of cutting or grafting a stem prior to aerial layering. A is a simple shallow wound. B and B1 show total and partial girdling. C uses a shallow cut to remove a sliver of bark and D shows a fine wire tied around the stem to cut the bark. E shows the finished layer packed in moist sphagnum moss and surrounded by firmly tied black plastic.

Grafting

If you have a large garden, there are few plants more spectacular than the fragrant, pink-flowered *Rhododendron griffithianum* hybrids. However, these plants and a few others can be difficult to obtain because they do not always grow well on their own roots and often have to be grafted.

'Cunningham's White' is the best commonly grown stock. It is preferable to *R. ponticum*, which was widely used in the past, because it does not produce basal suckers to the extent that *R. ponticum* does. It is easily propagated by cuttings or layers. Young, well-struck cuttings in pots are ideal as stock plants and one large specimen of 'Cunningham's White' should yield plenty of cutting material. Alternatively you may find a nursery that sells small plants suitable for use as grafting stocks.

These grafted rhododendrons are sitting on gravel in a container with a few centimetres of water. The container is usually covered with glass, creating a very humid atmosphere.

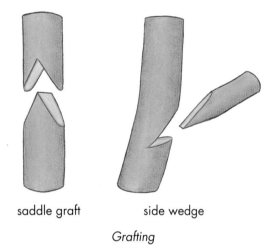

saddle graft   side wedge

Grafting

The best time to graft is in early spring as the sap starts to rise, but before the new growth begins to develop. Any grafting process requires that the cambium (the layer of cells below the bark) of the stock and scion (the variety to be grafted onto the stock) is kept in contact long enough to fuse and this involves some trimming and fitting to get a good match. The saddle graft and the side wedge are commonly used techniques that are quite easy to master.

The diagrams show the trimming and fitting methods for both. Practise making the cuts with a few old twigs before sacrificing any valuable plants. Bind the stock and scion

together with grafting tape if you have it, otherwise plumbers' thread tape or adhesive tape will do. This process is fiddly at first and takes some practice to master, but you'll soon get the hang of it.

Freshly grafted plants need to be kept in a warm humid environment to ensure good growth and to prevent the graft from drying. I find the easiest way to do this with potted rhododendron grafts is to line the bottom of a trough or tub with a few centimetres of gravel and then pour in water until it is just level with the surface of the gravel. The pots sit on the gravel and the water ensures that the atmosphere remains humid. If the trough can be covered with a few panes of glass, so much the better. Grafts in the garden should be covered with a plastic bag, making sure that the bag cannot dislodge the graft if it moves in the wind.

Once the scion is growing well and the graft has callused over, the tape can be removed. Do not leave this too long or you may find the tape starts to cut into the stem.

Chapter 9

HYBRIDISING

R. 'Unique'

DESPITE the many excellent species that are cultivated, keen rhododendron growers have always been hybridising their plants. Many hard lessons have been learnt and false trails followed over the years, but the breeders have persevered and we now have some excellent plants.

The process of hybridisation is nothing more than transferring pollen from one flower to another. In nature this is done by insects, the wind or in the case of primitive non-flowering plants the genetic material is transferred in water. The human hybridiser is just carrying out the normal natural process under more controlled conditions. In most cases the act of hybridising is easy; it is the waiting afterwards that is the hard part.

You will need a pollen parent and a seed parent. These are usually two different species or cultivars but some good hybrids have resulted from selfing, which is crossing a cultivar with itself. 'Trude Webster' ('Countess of Derby' selfed) is probably the most notable

example. If you have a pure species there is no advantage in selfing, unless you require species seedlings.

There are certain limitations that must be considered when selecting parent plants. Lepidotes cannot be crossed with elepidotes. Rhododendrons can be crossed with azaleas, but only with limited success. Elepidotes can be crossed with deciduous azaleas and lepidotes with evergreen azaleas. Although a few breeders have claimed success, evergreen azaleas are almost impossible to cross with deciduous azaleas. Vireya rhododendrons are not compatible with any of the other types.

There are also important genetic considerations, such as dominant colours and sizes. Almost any cross will include a plant with a dominant flower colour pigment, which can be expected to greatly influence the colour of the offspring. Crossing plants of disproportionate size will result in first generation offspring that tend towards one or other

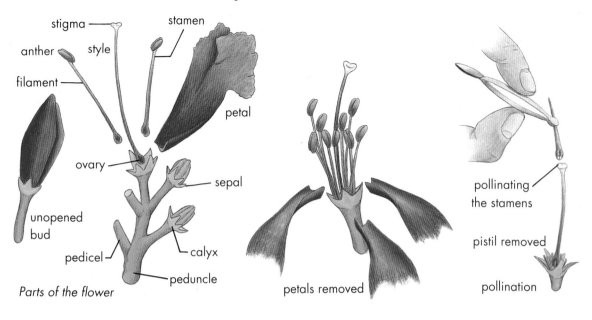

Parts of the flower

petals removed

pollination

extreme. In most rhododendrons, tall plants will be dominant in first generation crosses, but with evergreen azaleas dwarfness tends to dominate. The serious breeder needs to understand the genetic processes involved, but for the beginner almost any cross is going to produce something of interest.

For simple crosses you will need both the pollen and seed parents to be in flower at the same time. Freeze drying pollen or buying pollen already freeze dried can get round this problem. The most common method of freeze drying is to remove a few anthers from the pollen parents and place them in gelatine medicine capsules, which can usually be bought very cheaply from pharmacists. The capsules, which are semi-permeable and allow the passage of moisture, are then stored in a container of desiccant (silica gel is the most widely used) in a refrigerator, not in the freezer. After a week or so all the moisture will have been removed and the pollen can be stored indefinitely in a freezer. Allow the pollen to warm before use. For short-term storage drying by using the desiccant alone is sufficient. Dried pollen will last up to a year without freezing.

When choosing a flower to act as a seed parent look for one that is still closed but on the verge of opening. This will ensure that the flower is mature but unpollinated. Remove the unnecessary flower parts and pollinate using an anther from your previously selected pollen parent. It is not generally necessary to cover the freshly pollinated flower. Once pollinated, most flowers will not accept further pollen, but if you wish to be on the safe side a thin muslin bag tied over the flower will protect it from contamination. If the cross has been successful, the ovary of the seed parent flower should begin to swell noticeably within a week or so.

The process of selection begins as soon as the seed has germinated. Some sense of parental pride is important, but as far as rhododendrons are concerned there are plenty of hybrids out there, so cull ruthlessly. Hybridise with strict goals in mind and stick to them, record your crosses and the results and certainly do not expect any quick or earth-shattering results. Most important, have no qualms when it comes to culling excess numbers or consigning your lesser efforts to the compost heap.

With luck you may come up with something genuinely different and desirable. If

R. 'Sappho' has remained popular because of its unusual 'black and white' colour combination.

you do think that one of your efforts is particularly outstanding get it registered. Successful registration requires that a new hybrid is checked out to ensure that it would be a worthy introduction. Your local horticultural or rhododendron society should be able to provide details of the procedure required to register a hybrid. Don't worry too much if it never happens, most hybridisers find the exercise satisfying and worthwhile even if they never produce a plant suitable for register.

The problem is to sort out the best of the new releases. Old cultivars generally only tend to persist in cultivation because they have proved to be worthwhile but new cultivars often take many years before they prove their worth or show their faults. Parental pride often blinds plant breeders to the failings of their efforts; left alone, some hybridisers would produce whatever they fancied, but in order to survive nurseries they must produce plants that sell and that means giving the gardening public what they want. It is all very well for the real rhododendron buff to be impressed with an unusual new hybrid but real rhododendron buffs are rare crea-

tures. If the plant does not appeal to the masses the chances of a nursery keeping it in production are slim.

If a new variety is to survive and become a commercial success it must be virtually foolproof. Hybridisers with an eye to making the most from their endeavours are producing tough, easy-going plants with superior foliage and compact growth. While these never-fail plants may increase the gap between the rhododendron society enthusiast and the everyday gardener, I suspect neither side really objects to that.

Look at any grower's current list and you cannot fail to notice that although a few of the old benchmarks like 'Pink Pearl' are still there, modern hybrids raised from about 1955 onward predominate. There is no sign of the rhododendron market going back to earlier styles as has happened with old roses and perennials. Brighter colours in a greater range, compact growth, better foliage, greater disease and neglect resistance — the new plants have it all. Why go back? The real question is where to now?

GLOSSARY

R. mucronulatum

apical   At the apex or tip of a leaf or organ.

cambium   Thin layer of actively dividing cells which exists between the bark and wood of woody plants.

campanulate   Bell-shaped.

chlorosis   A yellowing of leaves caused by insufficient iron.

clone   A cultivar.

cultivar   Contraction of cultivation and variety. A plant produced by crossing two distinctly different parent plants and capable of being perpetuated only by vegetative reproduction.

dimorphic   Having two distinct forms.

elepidote   Without small scales on the leaves.

genus   A grouping of closely related plants that share certain characteristics.

glaucous   Bluish-green.

grex   (Latin: a flock, herd or troop.) Term used by hybridisers to describe groups of sister seedlings.

hose in hose   A style of bloom in which the sepals become petal-like and create the effect of a second corolla.

hybrid   A cross-bred plant.

indumentum   Felt or hair-like growth on the underside of rhododendron leaves.

lepidote   Having small scales on the leaves.

pH   A measure of the acidity or alkalinity of a solution.

scion   Shoot or twig of a plant used to form a graft.

selfing   Crossing a cultivar with itself.

species   A single plant type within a genus.

stock   A rooted plant into which a scion is inserted when grafting.

stomata   Minute openings in the epidermis of plants, especially on the undersurface of leaves.

subspecies   Naturally occurring self-perpetuating variation of a species.

tomentum   Hair-like growth on leaves or stems.

transpiration   Losing water, especially through the leaves.

variety   A normally non-self-perpetuating naturally occurring variation of a species.

vegetative propagation   Production of plants using vegetative (asexual) parts of the plant (stem, leaf, root) in contrast to sexual propagation in which plants are raised by seed.

ventricose   Having a swelling on one side; unequally inflated.

INDEX

Key: D = deciduous; E = evergreen;
  page numbers in italics indicate that
  the plant is illustrated.